DOONESBURY DELUXE

DOONESBURY BOOKS BY G.B. TRUDEAU

Still a Few Bugs in the System
The President Is a Lot Smarter Than You Think
But This War Had Such Promise
Call Me When You Find America
Guilty, Guilty, Guilty!
"What Do We Have for the Witnesses, Johnnie?"
Dare To Be Great, Ms. Caucus
Wouldn't a Gremlin Have Been More Sensible?
"Speaking of Inalienable Rights, Amy…"
You're Never Too Old for Nuts and Berries
An Especially Tricky People
As the Kid Goes for Broke
Stalking the Perfect Tan
"Any Grooming Hints for Your Fans, Rollie?"
But the Pension Fund Was Just Sitting There
We're Not Out of the Woods Yet
A Tad Overweight, but Violet Eyes to Die For
And That's My Final Offer!
He's Never Heard of You, Either
In Search of Reagan's Brain
Ask for May, Settle for June
Unfortunately, She Was Also Wired for Sound
The Wreck of the "Rusty Nail"
You Give Great Meeting, Sid
Doonesbury: A Musical Comedy
Check Your Egos at the Door
That's *Doctor* Sinatra, You Little Bimbo!
Death of a Party Animal
Downtown Doonesbury
Calling Dr. Whoopee

IN LARGE FORMAT

The Doonesbury Chronicles
Doonesbury's Greatest Hits
The People's Doonesbury
Doonesbury Dossier: The Reagan Years
Doonesbury Deluxe: Selected Glances Askance

DOONESBURY DELUXE

G B Trudeau

SELECTED GLANCES ASKANCE

INTRODUCTION BY STUDS TERKEL

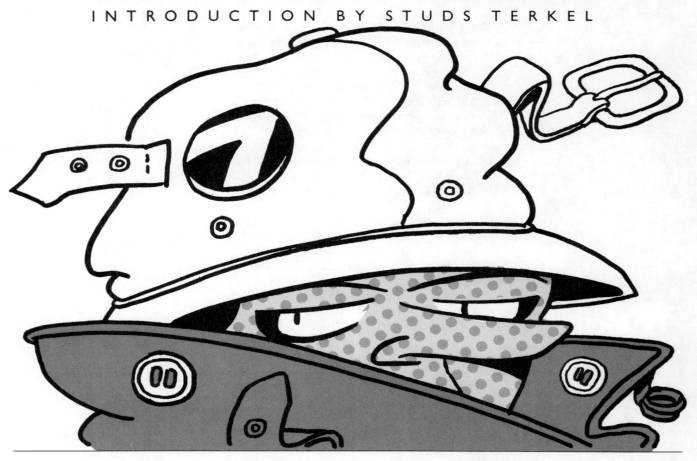

HENRY HOLT AND COMPANY / NEW YORK

For GF, with love

Copyright ©1984, 1985, 1986, 1987 by G.B. Trudeau
Introduction copyright ©1987 by Henry Holt and Company, Inc.
All rights reserved, including the right to reproduce this
book or portions thereof in any form.
Published by Henry Holt and Company, Inc.,
521 Fifth Avenue, New York, New York 10175.
Published in Canada by Fitzhenry & Whiteside Limited,
195 Allstate Parkway, Markham, Ontario L3R 4T8.

Library of Congress Catalog Card Number: 87-80724
ISBN Hardbound: 0-8050-0595-1
ISBN Paperback: 0-8050-0596-X

First Edition

Designer: Robert Bull Design
Printed in the United States of America

The cartoons in this book have appeared in newspapers
in the United States and abroad under the auspices of
Universal Press Syndicate.

1 3 5 7 9 10 8 6 4 2

ISBN 0-8050-0595-1 HARDBOUND
ISBN 0-8050-0596-X PAPERBACK

INTRODUCTION
BY
STUDS TERKEL

A funny thing happened to Garry Trudeau on his way to an honorary degree. It was at Grinnell College, 1977.

While the prexy held forth each diploma, dozens of graduates, some in cap and gown, others in blue jeans, stood sober ritual on its head. They danced toward the young cartoonist, shook his hand, and whispered things.

Seated next to him, I was astonished. Yet it seemed so natural, so matter of course. As they offered their regards to Joanie, Mike, Zonker, J.J., and the others of *Doonesbury*'s world, the ceremony took a half hour longer than usual. Nobody seemed to mind.

What makes the remembrance so indelible is the nature of Trudeau's work; it's indubitably political.

During the ensuing ten years, a stillness, for the most part, has descended on the American campus. Causes have become personal rather than communal; the official word accepted rather than questioned. Yet Trudeau's singular popularity among the young and their mellowed antecedents—the dancing graduates of that summery afternoon—is more impressive than ever. Nor has his social commentary ever been more trenchant.

Since the last *Doonesbury* anthology appeared, we've been tuned in to all sorts of strange music: televangelism's mega-million $ Te Deum; the contrabucks scandal; Grenada overcome; the drug-testing Olympics; Rube Goldberg's Star Wars; and Rawhide about to ride off the Oval Office movie set into a Hollywood twilight (if he doesn't forget).

These happenings, among scores of others equally surreal, have added a cockeyed dimension to the roller-coaster personal lives of Trudeau's people. As the baby boomers—say, Joanie and Rick—raise a kid of their own, this new person's first words are "although," "but," "unless," and "and." Orwell couldn't have put it any better.

There you have it: with a line or two, Trudeau makes clear what another might take a doctoral treatise to explain.

A book is yet to be written about our loss of tribal memory, the absence of our sense of history. Still, it may not be necessary. Consider Trudeau's despairing college prof challenging the somnambulism of his class: "The Constitution itself should never have been ratified. It's a dangerous document! All power should rest with the executive! What do you think of that?" The scribbling students awaken: "I didn't know half this stuff." Not a bad cautionary tale during this bicentennial year.

Free, easy, jazzy as a Johnny Mercer lyric; clean and minimal as a Basie piano; Trudeau's work breathes life into the Miesian doctrine: less is more. It is in this understatement that we recognize the hipness in the deadpan innocence of Mike Doonesbury and his circle; and that in the diversity within their sameness, we see the boomers as more than still life portraits. We see in their sometimes antic, sometimes poignant growing up the pursuit of a "goofy" ideal; or, at any rate, something better than what is. Reading *Doonesbury* offers a reed of hope as well as laughter.

IT CAME SPECIAL DELIVERY. MUST BE IMPORTANT.
IT'S FROM THE AGENCY..

FINALLY! THEY'RE ALL MOVED INTO THE NEW OFFICES AT THE WORLD TRADE CENTER! I START WORK ON MONDAY!

REALLY? HEY, WONDERFUL NEWS, MIKE! NO KIDDING! THE BEST!
IT SURE IS. SOMEBODY'S FINALLY BRINGING AN INCOME INTO THIS HOUSE.

I KNOW. IT REALLY TAKES THE PRESSURE OFF ALL OF US.
IT DOES NOT, ZONKER!

EXCUSE ME? HAVE YOU BEEN WAITING LONG TO SEE MRS. CONGDON?

OVER AN HOUR. SHE MUST BE PRETTY BUSY TODAY.
I GUESS. HEY.. YOU LOOK VERY FAMILIAR. DO I KNOW YOU FROM SOMEWHERE?

I DON'T THINK SO. MAYBE YOU KNOW MY WORK. I'M AN ACTOR.
THAT'S IT! I SAW YOU IN THAT NEW REAGAN COMMERCIAL! YOU PLAYED..LET ME SEE.. YOU PLAYED..

GOD.
RIGHT! YOU WERE GREAT! BOY, YOU'RE MUCH SMALLER IN REAL LIFE.

SORRY TO KEEP YOU WAITING SO LONG, MICHAEL. IT'S BEEN ONE OF THOSE DAYS.
OH, I UNDERSTAND, MRS. CONGDON. IT WASN'T ANY PROBLEM.

MICHAEL, I'D LIKE YOU TO MEET OUR PRESIDENT, MR. BELLOWS.
SO YOU WANT TO BE AN AD MAN, EH, SON?
WELL, I THINK SO, SIR..

I MEAN, I CAN'T BE CERTAIN, OF COURSE, BUT IT SEEMED WORTH LOOKING INTO, YOU KNOW, TO SEE IF IT WORKED OUT, IF IT FELT RIGHT AND.. I .. UH ..

TRY AGAIN, DEAR.
SO YOU WANT TO BE AN AD MAN, EH, SON?
YES, SIR. WITH A VENGEANCE.

MIKE, HERE'S THE POOP. OUR TOP ACCOUNT HAS JUST HANDED US A RUSH CAMPAIGN, AND I NEED A YOUNG COMER WHO CAN GET IT ON TRACK FAST. CASS HERE SAYS THAT YOU'RE MY MAN!

WELL, SIR, I'LL DO MY BEST NOT TO LET YOU DOWN. I'M VERY EXCITED ABOUT BEING A COPYWRITER, AND I'M ANXIOUS TO GET GOING!

AS LONG AS I'M SELLING SOMETHING I BELIEVE IN, I'LL GIVE YOU EVERYTHING I'VE GOT!
GREAT. I WANT YOU TO SELL RONALD REAGAN TO BLACK VOTERS.

I CAN'T STAND IT..
I SEE A CALVIN KLEIN APPROACH. RECLINING BLACK TEENAGERS TALKING ABOUT THEIR FIRST JOBS.

THE ECONOMY. ERA. ABORTION. DEFICITS. THESE ARE JUST SOME OF THE ISSUES GEORGE BUSH HAS REVERSED HIMSELF ON TO BECOME A REAGAN TEAM PLAYER.

TO SHELTER WHAT REMAINS OF HIS CONVICTIONS, BUSH IS ABOUT TO FORMALLY PLACE HIS POLITICAL MANHOOD IN A BLIND TRUST. AND HERE COMES THE VICE PRESIDENT NOW!

MR. VICE PRESIDENT! MR. VICE PRESIDENT!

YES.. ROLAND?

SIR, WILL YOUR MAN-HOOD BE EARNING INTEREST?

VERY LITTLE. THERE'S NOT THAT MUCH CAPITAL.

TODAY I AM FORMALLY PLACING MY MANHOOD IN A BLIND TRUST SO THAT I CAN CONTINUE TO SERVE RONALD REAGAN WITHOUT COMPROMISING MYSELF.

I SURRENDER MY MANHOOD WITH GREAT RELUCTANCE. AS I TOLD WALTER MONDALE, I'D LAY MY RECORD ON MANHOOD UP AGAINST HIS ANY DAY!

MR. VICE PRESIDENT, FOR THE RECORD, COULD YOU TELL US JUST WHAT YOU MEAN BY "MANHOOD"?

WELL, ACCORD-ING TO THE AMERICAN HERITAGE DICTIONARY..

THAT'S OKAY, SIR, I CAN LOOK IT UP.

YOU KNOW, THERE ARE SO MANY MARVELOUS POLICIES COMING OUT OF THIS ADMIN-ISTRATION, IT'S JUST A JOY TO SERVE THIS PRESIDENT!

BUT I DON'T THINK A PRESIDENT SHOULD EVER HAVE TO LOOK OVER HIS SHOULDER, ALWAYS WONDER-ING IF HIS VICE PRESIDENT HAS A MIND OF HIS OWN.

IT IS THUS A GREAT HONOR FOR ME TO SIGN THIS DOCUMENT PLACING MY MANHOOD IN A BLIND TRUST, TO BE ADMIN-ISTERED BY OLD FAMILY FRIENDS!

CLICK! CLICK! CLICK!

I'LL TAKE THAT PEN NOW, GEORGE.

YOU BET, MR. PRESIDENT!

MR. BUSH, WHY DID YOU DECIDE TO PLACE YOUR MANHOOD IN A BLIND TRUST INSTEAD OF SOMEWHERE ELSE?

WELL, IT WAS REALLY THE PRESIDENT'S IDEA. HE'S VERY MUCH IN CONTROL OF THIS WONDERFUL ADMINISTRATION, AND I RESPECT AND ADMIRE HIM FOR IT!

WHERE TO KEEP THE VICE PRES-IDENT'S MANHOOD IS JUST ONE OF THE TOUGH DECISIONS A PRESIDENT HAS TO MAKE. LBJ, FOR INSTANCE, USED TO KEEP HUBERT HUMPHREY'S MAN-HOOD IN HIS POCKET.

DID MR. REAGAN CONSIDER THAT?

YES, BUT WE AGREED A BLIND TRUST WAS MORE DIGNIFIED.

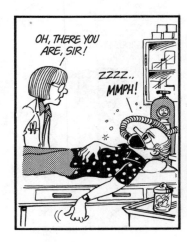

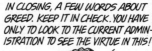

UM..CAN I GET YOU SOMETHING TO DRINK, ALICE?

NO THANKS, JEANNIE. I AIN'T THIRSTY.

NICE ROOF.

THANKS. WE LIKE IT.

SO. NICE DAY TODAY, ISN'T IT?

SEEN BETTER..

THE 5 TO 10 M.P.H. WINDS OFF THE RIVER PUSHED THE OVERNIGHT LOW TO 31°. IT FROZE ALL THE PUDDLES IN THE DOWNTOWN AREA.

TONIGHT WE'RE LOOKING AT PATCHY FOG AND SOME SHOWERS. FRANKLY, I CAN'T SEE HITTING THE EXPECTED HIGH OF 43° BY MID-DAY.

WEATHER'S AN IMPORTANT SUBJECT TO YOU, ISN'T IT, ALICE?

OH..I'M SORRY. WERE YOU JUST MAKING SMALL TALK?

ROBERT DIDN'T TELL ME YOU WAS SO NICELY PUT TOGETHER, JEAN.

HE DIDN'T?

PERSONAL APPEARANCE IS SO IMPORTANT, ISN'T IT? IT REALLY AFFECTS HOW PEOPLE TREAT YOU. HOW DO YOU GET YOUR LOOK, JANE? COULD YOU GIVE ME SOME TIPS?

UH..WELL, SURE. FIRST I TAKE A BATH.

ME, TOO.

OH, GOD.. I DIDN'T MEAN IT LIKE THAT.

WHAT ABOUT BEAUTY SOAP? DO YOU USE ANY SPECIAL BEAUTY SOAP?

SO, HOW'D YOU TWO GET ALONG?

JUST PEACHY, RON. WE'VE BEEN SWAPPING BEAUTY SECRETS!

IT TURNS OUT JENNY HERE HAS BEEN USING A SKIN TONER EVERY DAY FOR YEARS!

SHE HAS?

YOU DIDN'T **KNOW** THAT? HOW DO YOU THINK SHE GOT TO BE MORE BEAUTIFUL THAN LINDA EVANS?

YEAH, HOW?

SO **THAT'S** HOW YOU DO IT!

HUSBANDS AND WIVES NEVER TALK ANYMORE!

BAD NEWS, JANATA. INTERPOL HAS PICKED UP ON YOUR ROGUE SURGERY.

NO PROBLEM, NO PROBLEM.

NO PROBLEM? WHAT IS THAT, THE OFFICIAL THIRD WORLD SLOGAN?

THEY WOULDN'T DARE TOUCH ME, DUKE. I'VE JUST LANDED A MAJOR $1 MILLION GRANT TO PERFORM AN HISTORIC OPERATION!

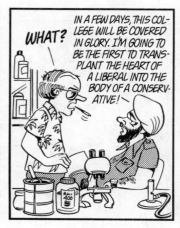

WHAT?

IN A FEW DAYS, THIS COLLEGE WILL BE COVERED IN GLORY. I'M GOING TO BE THE FIRST TO TRANSPLANT THE HEART OF A LIBERAL INTO THE BODY OF A CONSERVATIVE!

SURE. SOMEONE GAVE YOU A MILLION BUCKS TO BUILD A MODERATE.

ACTUALLY, IT'S MORE LIKE A COALITION.

JANATA, WHY THE HELL WOULD YOU WANT TO STICK A LIBERAL TICKER INTO A SICK CONSERVATIVE?

WELL, SOCIAL ENGINEERING HAS ALWAYS BEEN A PASSION OF MINE, DUKE.

I LOVE THE IDEA OF TAKING TWO IDEOLOGIES, ONE OF THEM PHILOSOPHICALLY ANEMIC, THE OTHER MORALLY BEREFT, AND BY FUSING THEM TOGETHER, CREATE A WHOLE NEW ORDER OF POLITICAL ANIMAL.

WHAT I HOPE TO GET IS A COMPASSIONATE PRAGMATIST, A MAN WHO OPERATES FROM A HYBRID SENSIBILITY OF ENLIGHTENED SELF-INTEREST.

WHAT IF YOU JUST GET A BIGOT WHO LIKES BRIE?

I'LL PULL THE PLUG. I TAKE PRIDE IN MY WORK.

JANATA, TELL ME. HOW DOES A FUGITIVE PLASTIC SURGEON FROM SRI LANKA BAG A BIG FOUNDATION GRANT?

EASY. HE STARTS WITH A GOOD IDEA.

THERE'S A LOT OF INTEREST IN BOTH TRANSPLANTS AND NEW POLITICAL HYBRIDS. THE TRICK IS TO ASK FOR ENOUGH MONEY SO IT APPEARS YOU KNOW WHAT YOU'RE DOING. THAT'S WHY I REQUESTED $1 MILLION.

ACTUALLY, I'VE ALREADY PERFORMED A SIMILAR OPERATION AT HOME AND BROUGHT IT IN FOR UNDER $3,000.

TIDY PROFIT.

OF COURSE, IN SRI LANKA WE HAVE NO TRADITION OF ANESTHESIA.

YOU KNOW, DUKE, THE POLITICAL TRANSPLANT TECHNOLOGY REALLY REPRESENTS A BREAKTHROUGH..

AT LAST WE CAN GET HARDHEADEDNESS WITHOUT HARDHEARTEDNESS INTO OUR POLITICS. IT'S A REPUDIATION OF THE IMPERFECTIBILITY OF MAN!

I DON'T KNOW, JANATA. SPENDING A MILLION SMACKS JUST TO CREATE ONE RETOOLED CONCERNED CITIZEN STRIKES ME AS SLIGHTLY INSANE.

COULDN'T YOU JUST START FROM SCRATCH?

SURE. GENE SPLICING. BUT YOU HAVE TO WAIT 18 YEARS TO FIND OUT HOW THEY'LL VOTE.

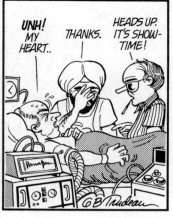

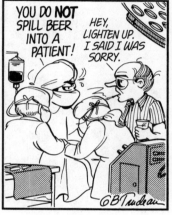

MIKE, HAVE YOU TALKED TO YOUR ATTACKER'S MOTHER YET?

OUT! OUT OF HERE!

C'MON, MIKE, GIMME SOMETHING! WHAT WERE YOU LIKE AS A KID?

OUT!

DO YOU OWN A HANDGUN, MIKE?

NO, BUT IF YOU PEOPLE DON'T STAY OUT OF MY HOUSE, I'M SERIOUSLY THINKING OF GETTING ONE!

WIN $500,000,000!
NEW YORK POST
FRIDAY FEBRUARY 7, 1985
Subway Hero vows:
"I'LL KILL AGAIN!"
Distraught Dad of none bares Death Wish details

TODAY A COALITION OF FARM BELT SENATORS PROPOSED A "WAY-OF-LIFE" LOAN PROGRAM TO SHORE UP THE NATION'S AILING FAMILY FARMS..

ALARMED BY THE ADMINISTRATION'S ANTI-SUBSIDY RHETORIC, BILL SPONSOR CHARLES GRASSLEY SAID THE WAY-OF-LIFE LOANS WOULD BE USED TO REFINANCE AN IMPORTANT PART OF AMERICA'S HERITAGE.

SENATOR, HOW WILL YOU DETERMINE WHETHER A FARM FAMILY IS ELIGIBLE FOR A WAY-OF-LIFE LOAN?

WELL, FIRST THEY MUST PROVE THEY STILL MAKE THEIR OWN CORNBREAD..

FROM SCRATCH?

MIKEY, HAVE YOU HEARD ABOUT THE WAY-OF-LIFE FARM BILL?

SURE, MOM. IT'S BEEN ALL OVER THE NEWS.

WELL, SENATOR NICKLES ASKED ME TO COME TESTIFY ON ITS BEHALF.

GEE. I DON'T KNOW, MOM. ARE YOU SURE OUR FARM REALLY QUALIFIES?

OF COURSE IT DOES, MIKEY. YOUR UNCLE AND I HAVEN'T HAD A PROFITABLE CROP IN YEARS. WE'RE FIGHTING FOR OUR LIVES, DEAR.

DO YOU THINK I SHOULD WEAR MY CALICO DRESS?

COULDN'T HURT.

YOUR MOM'S TESTIFYING BEFORE CONGRESS?

YUP. THE AGRICULTURE COMMITTEE. OUR SENATOR LINED HER UP.

APPARENTLY, HE REALLY BELIEVES SHE CAN HELP GENERATE SOME SYMPATHY FOR HIS WAY-OF-LIFE REFINANCING PROGRAM.

WHAT DO YOU THINK SHE'LL SAY?

I SHUDDER TO THINK. MOM'S BEEN THROUGH SOME PRETTY TOUGH TIMES, BUT SHE CAN LAY IT ON A LITTLE THICK.

STATE YOUR NAME, PLEASE.

THE WIDOW DOONESBURY.

NOW, MRS. DOONESBURY, YOU AND YOUR BROTHER-IN-LAW OPERATE A WHEAT FARM IN OKLAHOMA, CORRECT?

YES, THAT'S RIGHT.

COULD YOU TELL THIS COMMITTEE JUST HOW LONG THAT FARM HAS BEEN IN YOUR FAMILY?

YES, SIR. IT'S BEEN IN MY FAMILY FOR THREE GENERATIONS.

AND WHAT'S THE ONLY THING NOW STANDING BETWEEN YOU AND THE END OF YOUR WAY OF LIFE?

OUR CAR DEALERSHIP.

OH. WELL, THAT'S A WAY OF LIFE, TOO, RIGHT?

MRS. DOONESBURY, I HOPE YOU UNDERSTAND THAT WE ARE HERE TO EASE THE PLIGHT OF FAMILY FARMERS, NOT SO-CALLED WEEKEND FARMERS LIKE YOURSELF.

BUT THAT'S NOT FAIR! I WOULDN'T BE IN THIS MESS IF THE GOVERNMENT HADN'T URGED ALL OF US TO PLANT FENCE TO FENCE!

YOU AND THE BANKERS PUT ENORMOUS PRESSURE ON US TO TAKE OUT LOANS! MY BANKER HOUNDED ME DAY AND NIGHT! HE GAVE ME NO CHOICE BUT TO EXPAND PRODUCTION!

NO CHOICE, MRS. DOONESBURY?

HE OFFERED ME FLATWARE! 64 PIECES! WHAT WAS I SUPPOSED TO DO, THROW IT IN HIS FACE?

SENATOR, I REALIZE THERE'S A COMING SHAKEDOWN IN THE FARM ECONOMY, AND THAT THIS ADMINISTRATION WON'T DO MUCH TO CUSHION THE BLOW.

BUT THE FACT REMAINS I'M THE WIDOW OF A WORLD WAR II VETERAN, I'M THE MOTHER OF TWO, I BAKE APPLE PIE, AND I LIVE ON A FAMILY FARM! THAT SHOULD COUNT FOR SOMETHING!

I YIELD TO THE WITNESS'S AWESOME ICONOGRAPHY.

YOU BETTER.

JIMMY! I DON'T BELIEVE IT!

HOW'S IT GOING, STEVE?

WHAT ARE YOU DOING HERE, MAN? I THOUGHT YOU'D RETIRED!

WELL, I HAD. BUT I GOT TALKED INTO THAT ALL-STAR "USA FOR AFRICA" RECORD.

YOU DID THAT GIG? MAN, SEEMS LIKE EVERY OLD ROCKER IN AMERICA SHOWED UP FOR THAT SESSION!

YEAH. SOME OF THE NEW ONES, TOO.

HEY, GRAMPS! YOU LOOK FAMILIAR!

UH.. THANKS.

QUITE A NIGHT, EH, QUINCE?

I STILL CAN'T BELIEVE IT. EXCEPT FOR PRINCE NOT SHOWING, IT WENT OFF WITHOUT A HITCH!

IN ALL MY YEARS IN THIS BUSINESS, I'VE NEVER SEEN SUCH GENEROSITY AND COOPERATION BETWEEN MAJOR ARTISTS!

RING!

WELL, QUINCE, I THINK WE ALL JUST REALIZED THAT "WE ARE THE CHILDREN" IS A LOT BIGGER THAN THE SUM OF ITS PARTS.

IT'S PRINCE. HE SAYS HE'LL DO IT NOW IF YOU CUT OUT MICHAEL JACKSON'S PARTS.

SPEAKING OF CHILDREN..

WHERE'S YOUR YOUNG MAN, JOANIE? I THOUGHT HE WAS JOINING US.

I'M AFRAID HE'S ON DEADLINE AGAIN, LACEY.

THE PAPER HAS ASKED HIM TO WRITE A DAILY DIARY ABOUT HIS RELATIONSHIP WITH JEFFREY.

APPARENTLY, THERE'S A LOT OF INTEREST IN THE NEW BREED OF INVOLVED, HANDS-ON FATHERS.

DADDY?

NOT NOW, SON. DADDY'S BUSY.

TAP! TAP!

"MARCH 26 — JOANIE GOES TO VISIT HER MOTHER. I'M ON MY OWN WITH JEFFREY FOR THE FIRST TIME.."

TAP! TAP!

"AT 3:00 A.M., JEFFREY CRIES OUT IN HIS SLEEP. FROM WHAT JOANIE HAS TOLD ME, I KNOW THIS PROBABLY MEANS HE'S WET."

TAP! TAP! TAP!

"SO AS NOT TO WAKE HIM UP WITH THE LIGHT, I TRY TO CHANGE HIS DIAPERS IN TOTAL DARKNESS, A TASK ROUGHLY EQUAL IN DIFFICULTY TO TAKING APART AND REASSEMBLING AN M-16 IN A GUNNY SACK."

TAP! TAP!

" I DIAPER HIS HEAD."

TAP! TAP!

"MARCH 27 — I NOTICE TONIGHT THAT I SEEM TO HAVE DEVELOPED A SPECIAL RITUAL WITH JEFFREY."

TAP! TAP! TAP!

"EVERY AFTERNOON, JOANIE PICKS JEFFREY UP FROM DAY CARE. THEY GO TO THE PARK PLAYGROUND AND THEN COME HOME.."

TAP! TAP!

"JOANIE READS TO HIM, GIVES HIM A BATH, AND THEN AFTER DINNER, SHE BRINGS HIM TO ME WHILE I'M WATCHING THE NEWS, AND I KISS HIM GOOD NIGHT. I DO THIS EVERY NIGHT WITHOUT FAIL."

TAP! TAP! TAP!

" IT SEEMS TO WORK. JEFFREY'S TURNING OUT GREAT. "

TAP! TAP! TAP!

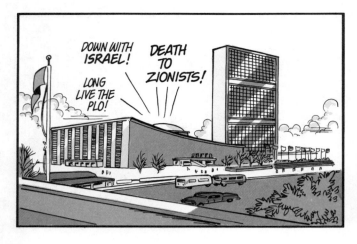

"MARCH 28—WHEN I COME HOME TONIGHT I FIND JOANIE IN TEARS.."

"SHE WAS UP LAST NIGHT WITH JEFFREY AND HAD TO CALL IN SICK AT WORK. JEFFREY'S BEEN THROWING UP ALL DAY AND STILL WON'T GO TO SLEEP."

"JOANIE SAYS SHE'S EX-HAUSTED AND DEMORALIZED. I TAKE JEFFREY AND TELL JOANIE THAT WE'LL SURVIVE THIS, WE ALWAYS DO, THAT ONE DAY WE'LL LAUGH ABOUT IT."

"MARCH 29-31 — AWAY ON BUSINESS."

".. AND AS I SHAKE TALCUM ON HIS TUMMY, I MARVEL AT WHAT A MYSTERY HE STILL IS, WHAT A MIRACLE. ALL THE WORK SEEMS WORTH IT TODAY."

RICK, YOU KNOW WHAT WOULD HAPPEN IF YOUR JOURNAL WERE WRITTEN BY A WOMAN? NOTHING. IT WOULD NEVER GET PUBLISHED. FROM A WOMAN, IT'D BE BANAL.

BUT YOU'RE A MAN. YOU'RE NOT *EXPECTED* TO THINK ABOUT ANY OF THAT STUFF! SO YOU CHANGE ONE DIRTY DIAPER AND IT'S A LITERARY EVENT!

"THE HARD QUESTION: HAVE I BEEN SLUMMING?"

FINALLY TONIGHT, WE TAKE A LOOK AT ONE OF THE MOST ENDURING RITES OF THE AMERI-CAN COLLEGE SCENE — SPRING BREAK IN FORT LAUDERDALE!

AS THE CITY BRACES FOR THE FINAL WEEK OF ITS SEASON, THINGS SEEM PRETTY MUCH AS THEY WERE 25 YEARS AGO. BEER-CHUGGING, WET T-SHIRT CONTESTS, AND CRUISING HIGHWAY A1A REMAIN AS POPULAR AS EVER!

AH, TO BE YOUNG AGAIN!

AH, TO BE YOUNG!

YOU GUYS GOT RESER-VATIONS?

ARE YOU KIDDING? THIS IS FORT LAU-DERDALE! JUST SQUEEZE US IN!

WELL, IF YOU DON'T MIND SHARING, I MIGHT HAVE SOME-THING FOR YOU.. LET'S SEE.. HMM..

THUMPA! THUMPA!

AH, YES. ROOM 201.

IS THIS *GREAT?*

YEAH.

DESPITE ITS RECENT DE-CLINE, THE MIGHTY DOLLAR WAS AGAIN THE SOURCE OF MANY HEATED DISCUS-SIONS AT THE ECONOMIC SUMMIT MEETING TODAY..

AFTERWARDS, THE PRESIDENT DEFENDED HIS COUNTRY'S BELOVED CURRENCY.

WE'RE PROUD OF THE FAITH PEOPLE PUT IN OUR DOLLAR..

FRANKLY, I THINK SOME OF THE MINISTERS HERE MAY BE JUST A LITTLE BIT JEALOUS OF MY MASSIVE DEFICITS.

MEANWHILE, IN TOWN, MRS. REAGAN CELE-BRATED THE STRONG DOLLAR IN HER OWN SPECIAL WAY.

HOW MUCH IS THAT?

.. AND AS WE STAND HERE TO COMMEMORATE THE 1945 LIBERATION OF THE CONCENTRATION CAMPS, WE MUST REMIND OURSELVES NEVER TO FORGET.

FORGETTING IS SOME-THING WE DO ALL TOO OFTEN. I KNOW THIS FROM MY OWN WAR-TIME EXPERIENCES IN HOLLYWOOD..

UH-OH..

I WENT THROUGH HELL MAKING SOME OF THOSE PICTURES, BUT YOU KNOW, FOR THE LIFE OF ME, I CAN'T REMEMBER WHO WON THE OSCARS IN 1945.

NO, NOBODY LIKES TO FORGET..

MR. REDFERN, THIS IS TOMMY DOWN AT SECURITY..

YEAH, TOMMY.

THERE'S SOME BAG LADY HERE TO SEE YOU. SHE GOT ON THE ELEVATOR BEFORE I COULD STOP HER.

WANT ME TO SEND SOMEONE UP?

THAT'S OKAY, TOMMY. I THINK I CAN HANDLE IT.

I BEG YOUR PARDON?

I SAID, SORRY IF I'M A BIT WHIFFY. THE COPS CLOSED THE HYDRANTS AGAIN.

WHAT A NICE SURPRISE, ALICE.

I GOT AN EVEN BIGGER ONE, ROG. GUESS WHO'S GET-TING HITCHED?

NO!

YUP. TO A FELLOW VAGRANT. WE FIGURED OUT THAT IF WE COMBINED OUR SOCIAL-SECUR-ITY, WE COULD ACTUALLY AFFORD A ROOM.

HE WAS AGAINST IT AT FIRST, BUT THEN HE BE-GAN TO SEE ALL THE ADVANTAGES OF POOLING OUR CHECKS.

AND YOU THINK YOU'RE COMPATIBLE?

OH, ABSOLUTELY. WE BOTH LOVE SHELTER.

"DO YOU, ALICE, TAKE ELMONT, TO HAVE AND TO HOLD, THROUGH SICKNESS AND HEALTH, 'TIL DEATH.."

WHAT?

EXCUSE ME, YOUR GRACE..

WE CAN'T PROMISE ALL THAT STUFF, HOLINESS. THIS BUM AND ME BARELY KNOW EACH OTHER. WE'RE JUST LOOKIN' FOR A WAY TO GET THROUGH THE NIGHT, Y'KNOW?

UM.. BUT THAT'S THE WAY THE SERVICE..

IF YOU'RE NOT UP TO THIS, DAD, GIVE ME THE BOOK!

ELMONT!

EXPRESS BUS TO UTICA! ALL ABOARD!

I CAN'T WORK UNDER THESE CONDITIONS.

"DO YOU, (INSERT BRIDE'S NAME), TAKE.."

EXCUSE ME? IS THIS THE CAMPUS COALITION FOR A FREE SOUTH AFRICA?

SURE IS. WHO ARE YOU?

SCOT SLOAN. I'M AN OLD MOVEMENT MAN. THOUGHT YOU MIGHT BE ABLE TO USE AN EXPERIENCED HAND.

EXCELLENT. JIMMY! LOG ME IN ON VOLUNTEER SCHEDULING.

I'M SY BRADLEY, BY THE WAY. I'M BLOCKADE MANAGER. HERE'S MY CARD.

CARD?

RAY! LET'S MOVE THE NEW DEMANDS ON THE WIRE! WE HAVE AN 0900 INTERFACE WITH TUFTS AND YALE!

..AND I HAVE YEARS OF EXPERIENCE IN ORGANIZING PROTESTS.

I'M AFRAID ALL OF OUR MANAGEMENT POSITIONS HAVE BEEN FILLED. HOW ABOUT BEING A FASTER?

A FASTER?

EITHER THAT OR I COULD WAIT-LIST YOU FOR THE BLOCKADE. I DON'T SEE ANYTHING ELSE HERE.

YOU DON'T SEEM TO UNDERSTAND, SON! I WAS AT SELMA! THE '68 PENTAGON MARCH! KENT STATE!

AND I RESPECT THAT. BUT NOBODY PUTS DAISIES IN GUN BARRELS ANYMORE.

I DON'T BELIEVE THIS.

HOLD IT, YOU OWN A BLAZER? WE NEED A HOST AT THE MEDIA CENTER.

EXCUSE ME, IS THIS SPOT TAKEN?

NOT AT ALL, REVEREND. PUT YOUR GEAR DOWN. YOU JOINING US IN THE FAST?

VEST OW!

IT WAS EITHER THAT OR BEING A MEDIA CENTER HOST. YOU'D THINK THAT AFTER PLANNING THE '69 MORATORIUM WITH SAM BROWN, I'D..

THE '69 MORATORIUM? YOU WERE THERE?

VEST OW!

IN SOME WAYS, I'M STILL THERE, SON.

WOW.. TELL ME ABOUT IT, REVEREND. TELL ME ABOUT THE MOVEMENT, WHAT IT TOOK TO LEAD THE ACTIVIST LIFE! PLEASE?

VEST OW!

WELL, OKAY. ONCE UPON A TIME, IN A LAND THEY SPELLED "AMERIKA"..

GOD, I'M GETTING SHIVERS ALREADY!

OUT OF SIGHT

LET'S CALL HIM TIMMY. WHILE HIS MAIN PREOCCUPATION AT THIS POINT IS CELL DIVISION, IN MOST RESPECTS, HE'S AS HUMAN AS YOU AND I.

WHAT HAPPENS WHEN HE IS ABRUPTLY SWEPT FROM HIS MOTHER? WHAT ARE HIS REACTIONS, HIS FEELINGS, HIS POINT OF VIEW? WE'LL BE TAKING A LOOK.

THIS PROGRAM SEEKS TO MAKE NO JUDGMENTS. OUR ONLY INTEREST IS IN PRESENTING THE FACTS ABOUT KIDS LIKE TIMMY AND LETTING THE VIEWER DRAW HIS OWN CONCLUSIONS.

BUT FIRST, LET'S TALK TO THE MURDERESS HERSELF..

TIMMY'S MOTHER. WALLOWING IN SELF-PITY, SHE EXPLAINS WHY TIMMY WILL NEVER SEE THE LIGHT OF DAY.

LOOK, HONEY, I'M UNEMPLOYED, UNEDUCATED, AND TOTALLY UN-PREPARED FOR RESPONSIBILITY.

WHY SHOULD I BE FORCED TO BE-COME A MOTHER UNDER THOSE CIRCUMSTANCES, ESPECIALLY WHEN THE KID'LL HAVE NO FATHER?

NO FATHER? BUT.. BUT HE WAS JUST CONCEIVED 12 MINUTES AGO!

EXACTLY. I SHOULD BRING A KID INTO A WORLD LIKE THIS?

AS THE MOMENT APPROACHES, TIMMY SEEMS ALMOST OBLI-VIOUS TO THE CHARGED DE-BATE THAT ATTENDS HIS FATE.

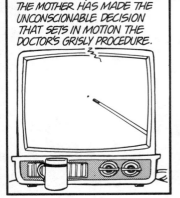
MINUTES LATER, THE DIE IS CAST. THE MOTHER HAS MADE THE UNCONSCIONABLE DECISION THAT SETS IN MOTION THE DOCTOR'S GRISLY PROCEDURE.

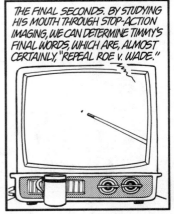
THE FINAL SECONDS. BY STUDYING HIS MOUTH THROUGH STOP-ACTION IMAGING, WE CAN DETERMINE TIMMY'S FINAL WORDS, WHICH ARE, ALMOST CERTAINLY, "REPEAL ROE v. WADE."

COMING UP: TIMMY REMEMBERED.

TIMMY MAY BE GONE, BUT HIS STORY IS PART OF ONE OF THE GREAT MORAL DEBATES OF OUR TIMES.

WE MUST FACE IT WITH CONVICTION. IF ABORTION AT **ANY** STAGE IS, IN FACT, THE TAKING OF A LIFE, THEN OUR REASONING MUST LEAD US TO A MONSTROUS CONCLUSION.

WITH 1.5 MILLION ABORTIONS BEING PERFORMED ANNUALLY, THE LEADER-SHIP OF THIS COUNTRY IS GUILTY OF TOLERATING NOTHING LESS THAN A HOLOCAUST.

OH, NO..

GOSH, THERE'S THAT WORD AGAIN.

SO HOW'S THE LAP OF LUXURY, SPORT? PRETTY CUSHY. I COULD GET USED TO THIS.

IS LACEY IN? AFRAID NOT, JOANIE. SHE'S ALREADY GONE OVER TO MAKE HER SHELTER PITCH TO THE DOWAGERS.

EVERYONE HERE LIVES IN HOUSES WITH NAMES LIKE "WINDSPRAY" AND "PEGASUS' BLUFF." I DON'T KNOW WHY MRS. D THINKS THEY'LL RELATE TO PEOPLE LIVING IN THE STREETS.

THAT'S AWFUL! WHY DON'T THEY JUST MOVE TO THEIR COUNTRY HOMES? CALM DOWN, DEAR. SHE'S GETTING TO THAT.

..AND WITH THE RIGHT PRIVATE SUPPORT, WE THINK THE SHELTER IN WASHINGTON COULD BECOME A MODEL FOR THE REST OF THE COUNTRY.

ALL IN ALL, I THINK YOU'LL FIND IT A VERY WORTHY PROJECT. I'M SURE WE WOULD, DEAR. BUT I DON'T KNOW IF IT'S FOR US.

IT'S NOT THAT WE DON'T CARE. AU CONTRAIRE, WE ADORE GOOD CAUSES. IT'S JUST THESE SHELTERS FOR THE HOMELESS HAVE A WAY OF ENCOURAGING VAGRANCY.

IF ONLY IT WERE AN ANIMAL SHELTER. OR A DISEASE. IF IT WERE ONE OF THE BIG DISEASES, I COULD HAVE A PARTY.

CONSUELA, I'M HAVING AN AIDE DROP OFF A COPY OF MY PROPOSAL TODAY. I HOPE YOU DON'T MIND. NOT AT ALL, DARLING. WHAT'S HIS NAME?

WILLY ROYCE. HE'S A PERFECT DEAR, AND A REAL FIND. HE USED TO WRITE POSITION PAPERS FOR JESSE JACKSON. JESSE JACKSON? OH, DEAR. YOUR AIDE ISN'T BY ANY CHANCE BLACK, IS HE, LACEY?

AS A MATTER OF FACT, HE IS. WHY DO YOU ASK, CONSUELA? I'M AFRAID HE MIGHT NOT GET HERE, DEAR. PALM BEACH HAS A TOWN LAW THAT'S A LITTLE..WELL, SPECIAL.

MY PASS CARD? YOU GUYS ARE KIDDING, RIGHT? WOULD YOU STEP OUT OF THE VEHICLE, PLEASE, SIR?

PASS CARD? OFFICER, THIS ISN'T PRETORIA. NO, SIR, IT'S PALM BEACH. ALL HOTEL AND DOMESTIC EMPLOYEES MUST CARRY I.D.'S.

SO? THAT'S THEIR PROBLEM. NO, SIR, IT'S YOURS. IF YOU DON'T HAVE AN I.D., THEN I'LL HAVE TO ARREST YOU FOR LOITERING.

LOITERING? HOW COULD I BE LOITERING AT 35 M.P.H.? I MEANT SPEEDING. IF YOU'LL GET OUT OF THE VEHICLE, PLEASE, SIR.

THIS IS DEFINITELY BECAUSE I'M BLACK, ISN'T IT? NO, SIR, HISPANICS ARE ENTITLED TO THE SAME TREATMENT.

WELL?

I'M DREADFULLY SORRY, DEAR. YOUR MR. ROYCE DIDN'T HAVE AN I.D., SO HE WAS DETAINED.

YOU MEAN, ARRESTED? FOR WHAT? FOR BEING AN UNDOCUMENTED BLACK MAN?

ORDINARILY, DEAR, IT'S A GOOD SYSTEM. IN FACT, OUR EMPLOYEES ALL LOVE IT.

IT GIVES THEM A SENSE OF SECURITY, OF BELONGING. THE CARDS MAKE THEM FEEL LIKE MEMBERS OF OUR BIG PALM BEACH FAMILY!

ARE THEY?

DON'T BE SILLY, DEAR. IT'S JUST SOMETHING THEY CAN SHOW THEIR FRIENDS.

©B Trudeau

CONSUELA, I HOPE YOU'LL MAKE MY GOODBYES FOR ME.

NOW, DEAR, I WOULDN'T MAKE TOO MUCH OF THIS LITTLE INCIDENT..

WE'VE REALLY MADE GREAT PROGRESS WITH THE RACES RECENTLY. WHY, IN 1979, WE DID AWAY COMPLETELY WITH AN ORDINANCE BANNING NEGROES FROM OWNING PROPERTY.

YOU DID THIS IN **1979**?

THAT'S RIGHT.

114 YEARS AFTER THE CIVIL WAR?

THEY SEEMED READY.

©B Trudeau

HIS NAME IS MR. ROYCE. WILLY ROYCE.

YES, MA'AM. HE WAS BROUGHT IN AN HOUR AGO.

ON WHAT CHARGE?

CHARGE?

YES, ON WHAT CHARGE WAS HE ARRESTED?

WELL, HE WAS AN UNDESIRABLE. I'M NOT SURE WHAT THE EXACT CHARGE WAS.

MAYBE YOU COULD **CHECK!**

HE WAS RIOTING OR SOMETHING. I KNOW WE CAUGHT HIM RED-HANDED.

©B Trudeau

HIS BAIL'S BEEN SET AT $500, MA'AM.

YOU WILL ACCEPT A PERSONAL CHECK, WON'T YOU?

I'M SORRY, MA'AM, WE CAN ONLY TAKE CASH.

HOW ABOUT COLLATERAL, THEN? I'LL LEAVE THIS DIAMOND BROOCH WITH YOU UNTIL I CAN HAVE THE CASH WIRED.

UH.. MA'AM, I DON'T THINK THAT'S ACCEPTABLE AS..

ACCEPTABLE? DEAR MAN, THIS BROOCH WAS GIVEN TO MY MOTHER BY THE DUCHESS OF KENT!

NO, I MEAN..

MOTHER ALWAYS TOOK IT WITH HER TRAVELLING IN CASE THE LOCAL CURRENCY COLLAPSED.

©B Trudeau

THE BAIL MONEY IS ON ITS WAY, WILLY. I JUST COULDN'T BE SORRIER ABOUT THIS WHOLE BUSINESS.

IT'S NOT YOUR FAULT, BOSS..

YES, IT IS, DEAR BOY. I SHOULDN'T HAVE ASKED YOU TO ACCOMPANY ME TO THIS INTOLERANT LITTLE BACKWATER!

NO, NO, IT'S ALL PART OF..

HOW HAVE THE AUTHORITIES TREATED YOU? HAVE YOU BEEN AFFORDED ANY SUSTENANCE SINCE YOUR ARREST?

WELL, NO, I..

GUARD! SOME COLD CUCUMBER SOUP, PLEASE!

NOW, SIP IT SLOWLY, DEAR BOY, YOU'VE HAD A DIFFICULT DAY.

LACEY, I ASSURE YOU I'M FINE.

WILLY, I'M JUST SO ASHAMED OF HOW SHABBILY YOU'VE BEEN TREATED HERE. I WAS UNDER THE MISTAKEN IMPRESSION THAT PALM BEACH HAD JOINED THE TWENTIETH CENTURY.

I'VE DECIDED TO CANCEL MY DINNER PLANS TONIGHT. I WANT YOU TO MEET ME HERE IN THE LOBBY AT 6:00, AND WE'LL GO DIRECTLY OUT TO THE AIRPORT. ALL RIGHT?

EXCUSE ME, SIR. ROUTINE CHECK.

WHAT?

MAYBE I SHOULD JUST MEET YOU AT THE CITY LIMITS.

OKAY, ENOUGH SUSPENSE, MICHAEL. IF HE'S NOT HERE ON VACATION, WHAT'S THE GREAT DOONES DOIN' IN HAITI?

HE CAME TO SEE YOU, GUY.

PSHAW!

IT'S TRUE. YOU SEE, ZONK, WE'VE GOT A NEW CLIENT AT THE AGENCY. THE AMERICAN CANCER SOCIETY.

THE AMERICAN CAN...?

TANNING. THIS IS ABOUT TANNING.

YOU GOTTA HELP US, ZONK. MILLIONS OF KIDS LOOK UP TO YOU.

WHAT? YOU WANT ME TO DO ANTI-TANNING ADS?

ZONKER, YOU'VE SAID YOURSELF TANNING IS DANGEROUS. THERE WERE 500,000 CASES OF SKIN CANCER IN THE U.S. LAST YEAR.

IF YOU, A FORMER PROFESSIONAL TANNIST, WENT ON THE AIR AND URGED KIDS TO GET OUT OF TANNING, THE IMPACT COULD BE ENORMOUS!

BUT..BUT I'M UNDER A LOT OF PRESSURE FROM MY STUDIES HERE! WHERE AM I GOING TO FIND THE TIME TO BECOME A T.V. STAR?

ZONKER, I CHECKED WITH YOUR DEAN. SCHOOL'S BEEN OUT FOR A MONTH.

SO THAT'S WHY THE TENNIS COURTS HAVE BEEN SO FREE!

WHAT DO YOU SAY? I COULD HAVE A CREW HERE BY TOMORROW.

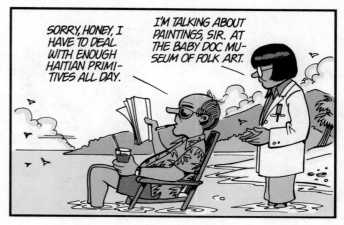

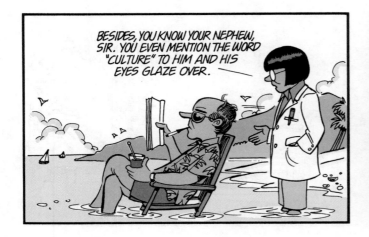

YOU KNOW, MIKE, THIS SINGULARITY CEREMONY MAY BE THE MOST POS- ITIVE STEP I'VE EVER TAKEN.

THE HARD PART WAS SIMPLY THAT I MAY WELL NEVER HAVE A PERMANENT PERSON IN MY LIFE.

AFTER THAT, I DISCOVERED A DIFFERENT MARCIA INSIDE. SHE'S STRONG, SELF-RELIANT, CAPABLE OF STANDING ON HER OWN. THIS NEW MARCIA RESPECTS HER- SELF.

HAVE YOU INTRODUCED HER TO YOUR PARENTS YET?

YES, AND THEY'RE CRAZY ABOUT HER. EXCEPT THAT SHE'S NOT JEWISH.

I DON'T KNOW WHY IT'S SO HARD TO FIND SOMEONE, MIKE, BUT IT IS. ALL THE GOOD MEN IN THIS CITY ARE EITHER MARRIED OR GAY.

NOW, MARCIA, THAT'S A BIT OF A CLICHE, DON'T YOU THINK?

IT'S ALSO A FACT. SEE THE HUNK IN THE JOGGING SHORTS OVER THERE?

WHERE?

HEY, JOGGING SHORTS! YEAH, YOU! WHAT'S THE STORY, MARRIED OR GAY?

BOTH.

SEE? IT'S JUST GETTING WORSE.

SEE YOU AT THE CEREMONY, MIKE. I'M GOING DOWN TO CLANCY'S TO HELP SET UP.

WANT ME TO WALK YOU THERE, MARCIA?

NO WAY, JOSÉ. PART OF BEING SINGULAR IS NOT BEING AFRAID TO GO TO PUBLIC PLACES ALONE!

YEAH, BUT IN YOUR UNDER- WEAR?

IT'S A LOOK, MIKE. I GOT INTO A NEW LOOK FOR THE OCCASION! TRÈS MADONNA, NO?

TRÈS. BUT WHAT IF YOU FINALLY MEET MR. RIGHT ON THE ELE- VATOR?

MR. RIGHT WOULD DRESS ME WITH HIS EYES.

OF COURSE HE WOULD.

FRIENDS, CO-WORKERS, AND EX- LOVERS: WE ARE HERE TODAY TO CELEBRATE THE END OF ONE OF THE MOST EXTENSIVE MANHUNTS IN THE HISTORY OF MANHATTAN.

TONIGHT IS AN OCCASION FOR NEW BEGINNINGS. AT THE STROKE OF MIDNIGHT, I WILL BE TAKING A SOLEMN VOW TO GET ON WITH MY LIFE!

IMMEDIATELY THEREAFTER, I WILL DECLARE AN OPEN BAR, PUT ON MY SHIRELLES TAPE, KICK OFF MY SHOES AND BOP 'TIL I DROP!

AT DAWN, I LEAVE FOR TIBET.

IN YOUR UNDER- WEAR?

YOU GOT BACK JUST IN TIME, HONEY. I'M GOING TO NEED YOUR HELP DURING THE MEDICAL CONFERENCE WE'RE HOSTING THIS WEEK.

THE COLLEGE IS HOSTING A MEDICAL CONFERENCE, SIR?

YEAH, ON ECSTASY. THE D.E.A., IN ITS WISDOM, HAS JUST DECLARED ECSTASY A BIG, BAD, SCHEDULE I NO-NO!

I DON'T THINK I'M FAMILIAR WITH THAT DRUG, SIR.

SHRINKS HAVE BEEN USING IT FOR YEARS, BUT THE KIDS, AS USUAL, RUINED IT FOR EVERYONE. THEY TURNED MDMA INTO A DAMN PARTY DRUG!

MDMA? OH, YOU MEAN METHYLENEDIOXYMETHAMPHETAMINE!

KNOCK IT OFF, HONEY.

YOU SEE, HONEY, ECSTASY IS A VERY PROMISING PSYCHOTHERAPEUTIC TOOL. BUT THANKS TO THE FEDS, THE WORK OF TOP MDMA RESEARCHERS HAS BEEN NIPPED IN THE BUD!

WHAT I'LL BE PROPOSING AT THE CONFERENCE IS THAT SOME OF THESE PEOPLE JOIN OUR FACULTY AND CONTINUE THEIR IMPORTANT WORK RIGHT HERE!

I SEE.

SIR, I HOPE THIS ISN'T JUST A FRONT FOR..

EVERY PENNY WILL GO TO SCHOLARSHIPS, HONEY.

SO WHAT'S THE HOLD-UP, DEAN HONEY?

THE STEWARDESS SAYS THEY WON'T GET OFF THE PLANE, SIR. THEY CLAIM THEY'RE HAPPY WHERE THEY ARE.

DAMN! I KNEW THIS WOULD HAPPEN!

WHENEVER YOU PUT A BUNCH OF HOT-SHOT DRUG DESIGNERS TOGETHER, THE FIRST THING THEY DO IS SWAP COMPOUNDS!

ANYONE HERE WANT TO HELP ME PROMOTE GOOD?

I DO! LET ME GET MY THINGS! IS THIS HOME OR ABROAD?

ON BEHALF OF BABY DOC COLLEGE OF MEDICINE, I'D LIKE TO WELCOME YOU ALL TO THE OPENING SESSION OF "ECSTASY: WHITHER THE FUTURE?"

I KNOW YOU SHARE MY OUTRAGE OVER THE OUTLAWING OF MDMA. WITHOUT UNFETTERED RESEARCH, WHERE WILL THE NEXT LITHIUM COME FROM, THE NEXT SACCHARINE?

SURE, THERE ARE RISKS, BUT THAT'S A SMALL PRICE TO PAY FOR PROGRESS!

SURE, THERE ARE RISKS, BUT THAT'S A SMALL PRICE TO PAY FOR PROGRESS! SURE..

UH-OH.

DR. GORP, HAVE YOU WORKED OUT THE ETHICAL RAMIFICATIONS OF MARKETING A DESIGNER DRUG AS UNTESTED AS "INTENSITY"?

NO, BUT MY TWIN BROTHER BUNNY HAS, RIGHT, BUNNY?

THAT'S RIGHT, ALBIE..

I'VE DONE A LOT OF RESEARCH ON THE MATTER, AND I CAN ASSURE YOU, MORALS-WISE, WE'RE ON TERRA FIRMA.

SIR, IF YOU HIRE THE SIDE EFFECT, I'M QUITTING.

NOW, DEAN HONEY, I CAN'T BREAK UP THE ACT.

A FIRST-RATE PRESENTATION, GORP, FIRST-RATE!

THANK YOU, PRESIDENT DUKE.

HAVE YOU THOUGHT OVER MY OFFER TO MOVE YOUR OPERATION DOWN HERE TO BABY DOC?

YES, I HAVE. I MIGHT BE INTERESTED.

GREAT. WHAT DO YOU SAY WE GO DOWN TO THE BEACH AND TALK TERMS?

SOUNDS GOOD.

YEAH, I COULD USE A DIP.

NOW, BUNNY, YOU KNOW YOU'RE WATER-SOLUBLE.

MICHAEL! WAKE UP! I'VE FINISHED!

HUH? WHA..? FINISHED WHAT?

MY SUITE OF PAINTINGS! TWO YEARS OF WORK FINISHED! IT'S OKAY FOR YOU TO GO INTO MY STUDIO NOW!

WHAT TIME IS IT?

I HOPE YOU CAN RELATE TO THEM. YOU'LL FIND A STRONG CURRENT OF IRONY CUTS ACROSS MY UNDERLYING COMMENTS ON KITSCH, SOCIAL POSTURING, AND.. AND.. OH, NO!

I FORGOT TO COMMENT ON CAREERISM. GIVE ME ANOTHER HOUR.

DAMMIT, J.J.! YOU'VE BEEN DOING THIS TO ME ALL WEEK!

OKAY, MIKE. THIS IS TWO YEARS OF WORK. SO I DON'T WANT YOU TO SAY ANYTHING AT FIRST. JUST GO INTO THE STUDIO AND SLOWLY TAKE IT IN, OKAY?

OKAY.

TWO WHOLE YEARS?

I TOLD YOU NOT TO SAY ANYTHING!

REMARKABLE! THAT'S THE ONLY WORD FOR IT.

YOU THINK?

ABSOLUTELY. WITHOUT ANY PANDERING AT ALL, YOU'VE MANAGED TO FUSE..UH.. ALL SORTS OF STUFF. YES, IT'S QUITE A FUSION!

IT SEEMS YOU'RE ON A THRESHOLD, RESTRAINED, YET RESTLESS. AUDACIOUS IN YOUR HANDLING OF..UH..YOU KNOW..THE..UH..

OH, HELL. WHAT AM I LOOKING AT?

NO, NO, GO ON! YOU ALMOST GOT IT!

BASICALLY, MIKE, THE FRAGMENTED SURFACES SPEAK TO THE VULGARITY OF RECENT IMAGE APPROPRIATION.

THEY CELEBRATE CONTINUITY WHILE DEPLORING THE STERILITY OF POST-GRAFFITI SOLIDISM. A COMMENT ON A COMMENT, IF YOU WILL..

OH.

ISN'T THAT OUR WEDDING CHINA?

THE VIEWER WON'T KNOW THAT. TO HIM, IT'S THE SHARDS OF THE AMERICAN DREAM.

YOU KNOW, MIKE, FINISHING MY SUITE PUTS ME AT SOMETHING OF A CAREER CROSSROADS..

ON THE ONE HAND, I COULD STAY PUT, PRESERVING MY REGIONAL AUTHENTICITY..

ON THE OTHER HAND, I COULD SWERVE INTO THE SOHO FAST LANE, CULTIVATE A GLITZY GALLERY REP, AND SELL MY PAINTINGS FOR $40,000 A POP.

OH, WHAT THE HECK. TAKE THE SECOND APPROACH.

YOU WON'T MIND BEING MR. J.J. CAUCUS?

SERIOUSLY? YOU WANT TO MOVE TO NEW YORK?

I THINK THE MOMENT HAS ARRIVED, MIKE.

BUT..

MICHAEL, I'VE FINISHED MY PAINTINGS. YOUR JOB'S IN NEW YORK. MY CAT JUST DIED. THE CAR BROKE DOWN. IT'S TIME!

RING!

HELLO?

HI, MIKE, IT'S YOUR LANDLADY. I'LL COME RIGHT TO THE POINT. I'VE SOLD THE HOUSE.

WHAT IS THIS, A MADE-FOR-T.V. MOVIE?

IT'S EVENTS, MIKE. THEY'RE OVERTAKING US!

THIS IS IT, FOLKS. A PERFECT FIRST APARTMENT!

THIS IS SO EXCITING, MICHAEL!

NORMALLY, THERE'S A LONG WAITING LIST FOR A CHOICE RENTAL LIKE THIS, BUT I LIKE YOU KIDS, SO I'M GONNA TAKE CARE OF YOU!

CLICK! CLICK!

GREAT SECURITY, HUH? THREE DEADBOLT LOCKS! WHO NEEDS A DOORMAN? COME ON IN AND CHECK IT OUT!

WOW! WHAT A CUTE HALLWAY!

WHAT DO YOU MEAN, HALLWAY?

YOU KIDS ARE GONNA LOVE THIS PLACE. IT'S VERY COZY, AND RIGHT NEAR THE SUBWAY.

IN THE SUBWAY IS MORE LIKE IT.

CLICK!

RUUMMBLE

BELIEVE ME, ONCE YOU SETTLE IN, YOU'LL HARDLY NOTICE.. HEY!

EXCUSE ME FOR A MOMENT, WILL YA, FOLKS?

I THOUGHT I THREW YOU PEOPLE OUT!

PLEASE, SEÑOR, THE BABY IS SICK..

MICHAEL, LET'S GO HOME.

THIS IS ROLAND HEDLEY, CUTTING SHORT HIS VACATION TO BRING YOU THIS EXCLUSIVE WHITE HOUSE REPORT.

TODAY IT WAS LEARNED THAT PRESIDENT REAGAN HAS AGREED TO MAKE A BENEFIT RECORDING FOR "USA FOR SOUTH AFRICA."

THE PROJECT, INITIATED BY THE REV. JERRY FALWELL, HAS ALSO ENLISTED THE HELP OF 25 OTHER CONSERVATIVE SUPERSTARS LIKE ED MEESE AND JESSE HELMS.

ALL PROCEEDS WILL GO TO BUY COMPUTERS FOR NEEDY SECURITY FORCES.

I'M ALSO PLEASED TO ANNOUNCE THAT SENATOR MALCOLM WALLOP HAS JUST AGREED TO JOIN THE OTHER CONSERVATIVE SUPERSTARS ON "USA FOR SOUTH AFRICA."

REVEREND FALWELL, WHAT WILL BE THE BASIC MESSAGE OF YOUR SONG?

PATIENCE. FAITH. TRUST..

ALSO, A RESPECT FOR THE FREEDOM OF PEOPLE TO LIVE HOW THEY CHOOSE, EVEN IF THAT MEANS LIVING APART. BEING APART ISN'T NECESSARILY AN INJUSTICE.

SO THAT'S WHY YOU'RE CALLING THE GROUP..

"APART-AID," RIGHT.

SO WHAT DO YOU THINK OF THE SCRIPT, B.D.? PRETTY EXCITING, HUH?

YEAH, BUT IT'S TELEVISION. YOU'VE GOT MOVIE CREDITS, BOOPSIE. WHY DO TELEVISION?

B.D., IT'S NOT JUST TELEVISION, IT'S "MIAMI VICE"!

DOING A "VICE" IS A REAL FEATHER IN AN ACTOR'S CAP THESE DAYS, EVEN IF THE PART IS PRETTY SMALL..

SMALL? BOOPSIE, THERE'S A SPORTS JACKET IN HERE THAT'S GOT MORE SCENES THAN YOU DO!

WELL, OF COURSE. THE JACKET'S A GUEST STAR!

WHAT'S THIS?

A "MIAMI VICE" TAPE. I GOT THE STUDIO TO SEND IT OVER.

I THOUGHT YOU SHOULD SEE FOR YOURSELF WHY IT'S SUCH AN HONOR TO BE ASKED TO DO THE SHOW.

OKAY, THIS IS DON JOHNSON, WHO PLAYS SONNY CROCKETT. HE'S THE ONE THAT MY CHARACTER FALLS FOR.

KIND OF SEEDY-LOOKING, ISN'T HE?

HUH?.. I MEAN, YES! I'LL REALLY HAVE TO ACT UP A STORM.

THAT'S THE STAR? DON'T COPS IN MIAMI SHAVE?

AND THAT'S HIS PARTNER, TUBBS!

YOU'D THINK A GUY WHO WEARS $800 SUITS WOULD BOTHER TO SHAVE.

IT'S A LOOK, B.D. IT'S CASUAL ELEGANCE.

OH.. LOOK.. THERE'S THE SHOW'S LOVE INTEREST..

THE LOVE INTEREST IS A CAR?

B.D., IT'S A WHOLE NEW CONCEPT HERE!

..AND THAT'S THE LIEUTENANT! HE GETS CHEWED OUT BY CITY HALL A LOT.

..AND YOU'RE SURE THE COLOMBIANS ARE DIRTY?

ARE YOU KIDDING, LIEUTENANT? WE EYEBALLED THEM MOVING 500 KEYS INTO THE BUNGALOW!

OKAY, LET'S MOVE!

WE'LL MEET YOU, THERE, LIEUTENANT. I GOTTA GO HOME AND CHANGE.

"CHANGE"?

SONNY ALWAYS WEARS MAUVE ON A BUST.

OH, NO! POOR SONNY! WHAT A TERRIBLE FALL!

HE SHOULDA SEEN THAT BIG JAMAICAN COMING!

OH, GOSH.. I HOPE HE DIDN'T TEAR HIS BELTRAMI PLEATED LINEN TROUSERS!

SAL, THAT'S NO REASON TO DROP OUT OF COLLEGE.

HERE COMES TUBBS! HE'S PULLING SONNY OUT OF THE BOUGAIN-VILLEA! HE'S BRUSHING HIM OFF..WOW, TALK ABOUT SUSPENSE!

AND THE BELTRAMIS ARE.. **OOO-KAY!**

OH, RIGHT. I'LL BET THEY USED STUNT PANTS.

PICK YOU **UP?** SAL, I JUST DROPPED YOU OFF!

IT'S MY ROOM-MATE, MAN. THEY ASSIGNED ME A MAJOR FLAMER!

SAL, THAT'S NO REASON TO DROP OUT OF COLLEGE.

IT'S JUST NOT WORKING, MAN! I DON'T FIT IN! I GOTTA GET OUTTA HERE!

SAL, EVERY-ONE FEELS THAT WAY THE FIRST FEW WEEKS..

DAMMIT, MIKE! THIS IS AN EMER GENCY!

HOW ABOUT ONE MORE RUBBER, GENTS?

EXCEL-LENT!

SAL, LET'S GO TALK THIS OUT FIRST, OKAY?

I'M TELLING YOU, MAN, THE GUY'S A WORLD-CLASS FLAMER! I CAN'T TAKE ONE MORE **DAY** HERE!

SAL, EVERYBODY HAS ROOMMATE PROBLEMS. IT'S PART OF BEING IN..

HI, HO! COMPANY?

HI, I'M SAL'S BROTHER, MIKE DOONES-BURY.

TRIP TRIPLER.. NICE TO MEET YOU, MR. DOONESBURY.

MR. DOONES-BURY?

WHY, YES, SIR. YOU'RE MY ELDER, AREN'T YOU?

SEE WHAT I MEAN?

SAL, I'M SURE IF YOU GUYS JUST TALK IT OUT..

MIKE, BELIEVE ME, THE FLAMER AND I HAVE **NOTHING** TO TALK OUT!

TOO BAD, IN A WAY. IN THE NEW OP-PORTUNITY SOCIETY, THERE'S ROOM FOR EVERYONE! SOME PEOPLE JUST HAVEN'T CAUGHT ON THAT IT'S **MORNING** IN AMERICA!

LOOK, TO BEGIN WITH, I'M NOT A MORNING PERSON..

YOU'LL NEVER MAKE AN EN-TREPRENEUR, SLEEPY HEAD!

OKAY, DR. DAN, BE-SIDES GUM DISEASE, WHAT *ELSE* ARE THE BIG CHILL CHILDREN TALKING ABOUT THESE DAYS?

BALD-NESS, MARK.

BOY BOOMERS DON'T SEEM TO BE ABLE TO HANDLE THINNING HAIR. THEY THOUGHT THEY'D BE YOUNG FOREVER.

THEY'RE TRYING EVERYTHING: MINOXIDIL, CONDITIONERS, NEW HAIR STYLES. MANY ARE REGROWING THE BEARDS OF THEIR YOUTH. THIS IS NOT A GENERATION THAT'S AGING GRACEFULLY.

OKAY, BESIDES HAIR LOSS AND GUM DISEASE..

THAT'S ABOUT IT. THERE'S SORT OF A LULL.

DR. D, WHY DO YOU FEEL THE BOOMERS ARE SO OBSESSED WITH THE PROB-LEMS OF AGING?

BECAUSE THEIR GENERATIONAL IDENTITY HAD SO MUCH TO DO WITH YOUTH, MARK.

YOU PRESS A 38-YEAR-OLD BABY BOOMER, AND HE'LL USUALLY ADMIT THAT IN HIS HEART OF HEARTS HE STILL THINKS OF HIMSELF AS A "KID."

BUT DON'T YOU THINK THAT HAV-ING THEIR *OWN* KIDS IS FINALLY MAKING THE BOOM-ERS GROW UP?

YEAH, THAT PLUS YOU'RE STARTING TO SEE THE FIRST BOOMER HEART ATTACKS.

THAT'LL DO IT.

HEY, LET'S FACE IT. HAVING A CORONARY IN YOUR BLUE JEANS IS EMBARRASSING.

DR. DAN, WHAT ABOUT THAT NOTORIOUS BABY BOOM SUBSPECIES — THE YUPPIE? IS HE A PHENOMENON OF THE PAST?

WELL, AS AN OBJECT OF MEDIA INTEREST, THERE'S NO QUESTION HE'S IN REMISSION.

THE YUPPIE'S VERY RESILIENT, THOUGH. I HAVE NO DOUBT HE'LL BE BACK, PROBABLY IN TIME FOR THE CHRISTMAS SEASON. HE TENDS TO RE-APPEAR IN CYCLES.

HE SOUNDS LIKE A FRUIT FLY.

HE'S BEEN CALLED WORSE.

YOU SEE, MARK, A TRULY COHESIVE GENERATION ONLY COMES ALONG ONCE OR TWICE A CENTURY. THAT'S WHY THE BOOMERS WILL BE TRACKED FOR THE REST OF THEIR LIVES.

THIS GENERATION IS LIKE A GREAT COMET, BLAZING THROUGH THE FIRMAMENT, CARRYING WITH IT A DREAM AS BOUNDLESS AS THE UNI-VERSE ITSELF!

WHEW..

HOW WILL WE KNOW WHEN IT'S OVER?

"ESQUIRE" WILL RUN A PIECE ON THE HOT NEW FUN-ERAL HOMES.

PART

TWO

SAL? DEPENDS. WHO'S ASKIN'?

SCOT SLOAN! I'M THE UNIVERSITY CHAPLAIN. YOUR BROTHER ASKED ME TO LOOK IN ON YOU. WHAT FOR, MAN?

TO HELP YOU ADJUST, GET YOU INTEGRATED INTO THE LIFE OF THE COMMUNITY. HI, HO! COMPANY? EXCELLENT!

COULD YOU DO HIM FIRST? I'M RUNNIN' LATE. UH-OH! A MAN OF THE CLOTH! HIDE THE ASH-TRAYS! JUST KIDDING.

SAL, MIKE SAYS YOU'RE HAVING PROBLEMS FITTING IN HERE. WHO WANTS TO FIT IN, MAN?

YOU WANT ME TO FIT IN WITH MY ROOMMATE AND ALL THE OTHER PRE-MED FLAMERS, THE CLASS OF THE LIVING DEAD?

THE WHOLE ATMOSPHERE HERE STINKS, MAN. THE ADMINISTRATION, THE FACULTY, THEIR LUNCHMEAT COURSES, THEY ALL STINK! THIS PLACE MAKES ME PUKE!

SAL, WHY ARE YOU HERE? BEATS HOME, MAN.

YOU KNOW, SAL, I'M SENSING THAT YOUR PROBLEM IS A LACK OF A PERSONAL PHILOSO-PHY. GET OUTA HERE, MAN. I GOT A PHILOSO-PHY!

BASICALLY, I BELIEVE WE WERE PUT HERE TO PARTY. AND I MEAN, PARTY! WHEN THE ACTION COMES DOWN, IT'S GOTTA BE JUST TOTALLY OUTA HAND OR I PASS!

THE IMPORTANT THING IS NOT TO CARE. THAT WAY, WHEN THINGS GET OLD, AS THEY FREQUENTLY DO, I'M GONE, BUT I'M NOT STRESSED OUT.

THAT'S A PHILOSOPHY? WELL, IT'S NOT LIKE PUBLISHED OR ANYTHING.

SAL, HAVE YOU CON-SIDERED THE CHURCH AS A WAY OF COMING TO TERMS WITH SOME OF YOUR PROBLEMS? NO WAY, DUDE!

THE GOD THING DOESN'T MAKE IT FOR ME, OKAY? LOOK AT WHAT RELIGION'S GIVEN US— INQUISI-TIONS, PERSECUTIONS, "HOLY" WARS, AND NOW TERRORISM!

I JUST CAN'T GET INTO SOME MACHO GOD WITH HIS OWN PRI-VATE SENSE OF JUSTICE THAT PERMITS HIM TO SLAUGHTER THE EVIL AND INNOCENT ALIKE!

YOU MAKE HIM SOUND LIKE DIRTY HARRY. I JUST THINK HE SHOULD LIGHTEN UP, Y'KNOW?

SO IS SUPERFLY GOING TO HELP WITH THE LOBBY TREE?

HE GAVE ME A $100 BILL JUST TO GET RID OF ME. HE DIDN'T EVEN WANT CHANGE.

THAT GUY'S GOT IT WIRED.. HE JUST SITS IN HIS APARTMENT WHILE AN ENDLESS STREAM OF PEOPLE BRING HIM LARGE AMOUNTS OF CASH.

MEANWHILE, WORKING STIFFS LIKE ME HAVE TO PUT IN 12-HOUR DAYS TO BE ABLE TO AFFORD TO LIVE IN A BUILDING WITH NEIGHBORS LIKE HIM!

THERE'S JUST NO JUSTICE IN THE..

CLICK!

COMING UP, A CARIBBEAN MED STUDENT WINS $23 MILLION.

SIR! WAKE UP! YOU'RE MISSING ALL THE EXCITEMENT!

WHAT?.. >SNORT!< WHAT EXCITEMENT?

ZONKER'S PRESS CONFERENCE ON HIS LOTTERY PRIZE!

HE GOT SO MANY CALLS FROM THE MEDIA THIS WEEKEND, HE DECIDED TO READ A PREPARED STATEMENT ABOUT HIS PLANS.

"..AND, OF COURSE, I'LL BE DATING SHOW GIRLS."

BEFORE THE CHECK CLEARS?

ZONKER! HOW DID YOU FEEL WHEN YOU HEARD THE GOOD NEWS?

YEAH, WHAT WERE YOUR FEELINGS?

COULD YOU DESCRIBE THEM?

WELL, AT FIRST I DIDN'T FEEL ANYTHING. I JUST WENT NUMB.

THEN I FELT A RUSH OF GIDDINESS, FOLLOWED BY FEELINGS OF DISORIENTATION, QUEASINESS, SHORTNESS OF BREATH..

..HUNGER, RAGE, SEXUAL LONGING, VERTIGO, BOREDOM, AND FINALLY, A TINGLING SENSATION.

WHAT ABOUT AFTER THE NEWS SUNK IN?

LADIES AND GENTLEMEN, THE BOTTOM LINE HERE IS THAT NO AMOUNT OF MONEY COULD EVER INTERFERE WITH MY DREAM OF ESTABLISHING A PRIVATE MEDICAL PRACTICE IN SOUTHERN CALIFORNIA.

WHAT ABOUT CHARITY, ZONKER?

HOW DOES YOUR FAMILY FEEL?

WHAT'S THE TAX BITE?

HEY, HEY, YOU NETWORK BOYS HAVE BEEN HOGGING ALL THE QUESTIONS. LET'S LET THE SUPERMARKET MEDIA GET IN A FEW, OKAY?

ZONKER, ABOUT YOUR LOVE-CHILD WITH MRS. GORBACHEV..

ZONKER, WILL YOU BE SLAYING MOM, CO-ED, SELF?

THAT'LL HAVE TO BE THE LAST QUESTION, BOYS! I HAVE TO GET BACK AND HIT THE BOOKS!

SO SAID LOTTERY WINNER ZONKER HARRIS THIS MORNING AS HE RETURNED TO CLASSES HERE AT THE ACADEMICALLY GRUELING BABY DOC COLLEGE OF PHYSICIANS.

$23 MILLION JUST DOESN'T SEEM TO HAVE CHANGED THIS UNAFFECTED YOUNG MAN AND HIS BOYHOOD DREAM OF BECOMING A DOCTOR.

YO, BABE! I'LL GIVE YOU TEN GRAND TO TAKE MY BIO-CHEM EXAM!

OKAY.

GB Trudeau

WHO YOU CALLING, MIKE?

ZONKER. NOW THAT HE'S RICH, I THOUGHT HE MIGHT BE ABLE TO FLY UP FOR OUR FAREWELL PARTY AT WALDEN.

HE'S PROBABLY TOO IMPORTANT NOW TO TAKE YOUR CALL.

ZONKER? OH, COME ON, J.J.!

PEOPLE CHANGE, MIKE.

HI, ZONKER HARRIS SPEAKING!

ZONK? HI, BUDDY, IT'S..

ALL MY OPERATORS ARE BUSY RIGHT NOW, BUT IF YOU'LL HOLD..

GB Trudeau

LISTEN, ZONK, THE REASON I CALLED IS THAT WE'RE MOVING OUT OF WALDEN NEXT WEEK AND WE'VE DECIDED TO HAVE A FAREWELL REUNION.

SINCE YOU CAN AFFORD IT NOW, J.J. AND I WERE HOPING YOU'D BE ABLE TO FLY UP AND JOIN US FOR THE FESTIVITIES!

I WOULDN'T MISS IT, MIKEY. IT'S A LOVELY GESTURE TO ASK ME. YOU'RE STILL MY FRIEND OF FRIENDS.

WELL, OF COURSE I AM.

BOY, I HOPE I DON'T OUTGROW YOU, MAN!

ME, TOO, ZONK.

GB Trudeau

I GOT THE RICKSHAW ALL WARMED UP TO TAKE YOU TO THE AIRPORT, LAD!

UNCLE DUKE, I DON'T WANT A RICKSHAW.

THEN I'LL HAVE THE LIMO SENT ROUND. LET ME GIVE YOU A HAND HERE.

YOU CERTAINLY ARE BEING CONSIDERATE, UNCLE DUKE.

THANKS, NEPHEW.

A TEENY BIT OUT OF CHARACTER, WOULDN'T YOU SAY?

YOU'RE RIGHT. WANT ME TO SEE A SHRINK? I WILL IF YOU'RE WORRIED.

GB Trudeau

.. AND I TALKED TO NICHOLE LAST WEEK. SHE SENDS HER LOVE.

SORRY I CAN'T BE WITH YOU, GENTS. PAT THE HOUSE GOOD-BY FOR ME.

IT'S ABOUT *TIME* YOU MOVED OUT OF THAT DUMP!

ALL PRESENT AND ACCOUNTED FOR IN SPIRIT.

NOW YOU'VE DONE IT. HERE COME THE TOURISTS.

Walden Commune 1972-1985

GEE, MISTER, DID YOU REALLY USED TO LIVE IN A COMMUNE?

Walden Commune 1972-1985

I SURE DID, YOUNGSTER.

GOSH! WHAT WAS IT LIKE?

Walden Commune 1972-1985

WHAT WAS IT LIKE? WELL, THAT'S A LONG STORY, SON. THE THINGS WERE VERY DIFFERENT BACK THEN.

Walden Commune 1972-1985

"TO BEGIN WITH, IT WAS AN AGE OF INNOCENCE.."

OKAY, SAY PAUL *IS* DEAD..

OH, WOW, I SEE WHAT YOU MEAN!

HEY, EVER LOOKED AT YOUR HANDS? LIKE *REAL-LY* LOOKED AT YOUR HANDS?

"WHAT WAS WALDEN? WELL, SON, IT WAS ABOUT SHARING.."

GO AHEAD, THEY'RE YOURS! I KNOW YOU LOVE THESE BELLBOTTOMS, MIKE!

".. IT WAS ABOUT PERSONAL GROWTH.."

I.. I THINK I'M READY TO GET IN TOUCH WITH MY FEMININE SIDE.

OH, B.D., I *KNEW* YOU'D COME AROUND!

".. AND PRINCIPLED ACTIVISM."

NOT YET. IT'S HARD TO RE-PUDIATE INTERVEN-TIONISM WITHOUT SEEMING TO CHAM-PION OPPOSING VALUES.

WORKED OUT A SLOGAN YET, MIKE?

OF COURSE, IT WASN'T *ALL* MORAL GLAMOUR..

ZZZZ!

Walden Commune 1972-1985

..AND THE LADIES' ROOM WILL BE COVERED WITH THESE DAY-GLO DOODLES. THE IDEA IS TO IMPART A SENSE OF FUN TO TYPICALLY STERILE SURROUND-INGS.

THE MEN'S ROOM WILL BE EVEN MORE INTERACTIVE. LET ME SHOW YOU MY CON-CEPT FOR THE URINALS.

THE URINALS NEED A CONCEPT?

I'M INSTALLING THEM IN OLD TV'S LIKE THIS. IT WILL COMPEL THE USER TO COME TO TERMS WITH HIS FEELINGS ABOUT MASS CULTURE!

PWACK!

WHOOSH!

GURGLE

J.J., AS A LONG-TIME USER..

AND TO MAKE THE EXPERIENCE MORE THEATRICAL, I'M FILLING THEM WITH DRY ICE.

SSSSSSS!

GB Trudeau

WELL, IT SEEMS J.J. JUST GOT HER FIRST COMMISSION!

OH, YEAH?

SHE'S DESIGNING THE REST ROOMS FOR SOME SORT OF CLUB IN THE EAST VILLAGE!

IT SOUNDS WILD, ESPECIALLY HER CONCEPT FOR THE TOILET STALLS!

HOW DOES IT FLUSH?

JUST POP THE CLUTCH.

GB Trudeau

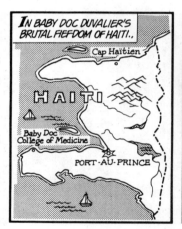

IN BABY DOC DUVALIER'S BRUTAL FIEFDOM OF HAITI..

Cap Haïtien

HAITI

Baby Doc College of Medicine

PORT-AU-PRINCE

..WHERE THE SECRET RITES OF VODOUN ARE PRACTICED MUCH AS THEY WERE 200 YEARS AGO..

..A SOUL-SEARING SCREAM PIERCING THE STILL OF THE NIGHT..

AAIEE!

..HARDLY RAISES AN EYEBROW.

KEEP IT DOWN, SIR!

GB Trudeau

CARRIED ALONG BY GENTLE TRADE WINDS OFF HAITI..

..A SOLITARY FLY..

..BEGINS HIS DAY.

BZZZZZ!

SIR? SIR?

GB Trudeau

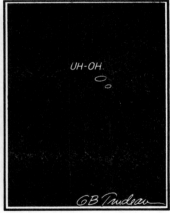

THUMP! THUMP!

OKAY, THE DOOR'S STUCK, BUT I THINK THAT'S THE DEN.

OKAY, THE STAIRS ARE BLOCKED, BUT TAKE MY WORD FOR IT, THERE'S A FULLY APPOINTED BATHROOM UP THERE!

BASICALLY, WHAT WE HAVE HERE IS THE PERFECT FIXER-UPPER, AND IN A NEIGHBORHOOD THAT'S STILL UNDISCOVERED!

YOU KIDS WOULD BE GETTING IN ON THE GROUND FLOOR. YOU'D BE PUTTING DOWN ROOTS IN AN AREA OF NEW YORK THAT'S STILL PRIMITIVE AND UNSPOILED.

I DON'T LIKE THE SOUND OF THAT..

C'MON, MICHAEL, HE JUST MEANS IT HASN'T BECOME INFESTED WITH COOKIE BOUTIQUES YET.

THAT'S RIGHT, MR. DOONESBURY. YOU'D BE AUTHENTIC HOMESTEADERS, CARVING A NEW LIFE FOR YOURSELVES IN A COMMUNITY OTHERS HAVE GIVEN UP ON!

AND YOU'RE SURE WE'RE NOT TOO LATE?

POSITIVE. ALL YOU NEED IS A LITTLE IMAGINATION!

..AND HERE HE IS, THE **REAL** GEORGE BUSH!

BUT DON'T BLINK!

HEE, HEE!

LET ME MAKE A SMALL CONFESSION HERE..

WHEN MY CAMPAIGN ADVISORS FIRST BRIEFED ME ON SOME OF MY NEW POSITIONS, I MUST SAY I THOUGHT THEY WERE A LITTLE EXTREME..

BUT THEN I GOT TO KNOW SOME OF YOU IN THE NEW RIGHT, AND I SAW THAT GOLDWATER WAS CORRECT: EXTREMISM IN THE DEFENSE OF LIBERTY IS NO VICE!

WHEN MY CRITICS ACCUSE ME OF "PANDERING TO THE NUTS," I ASK THEM, WHAT'S WRONG WITH BEING NUTS ABOUT AMERICA? WHAT'S WRONG WITH BEING NUTS ABOUT THE FLAG?

IT'S **EXACTLY** THAT KIND OF NUTTINESS THAT MADE THIS COUNTRY GREAT! AND BY GOLLY, THAT'S WHY I'M A NUT ABOUT ALL OF YOU! THANKS VERY MUCH.

THANK **YOU**, MR. VICE PRESIDENT. SHALL WE SET UP THE HOOPS NOW?

I LOVE THIS PART.

YOU AND J.J. HAVE REALLY CARVED OUT AN AWESOME NEW LIFESTYLE FOR YOURSELVES, MIKE.

OH, I DON'T KNOW ABOUT THAT, Z..

EVER WONDER WHAT'S BECOME OF WALDEN SINCE YOU LEFT?

WELL, ACTUALLY..

CONDOS IS MY GUESS. WHAT ELSE? THIS IS THE EIGHTIES. IT HAS TO BE CONDOS, RIGHT?

WRONG.

PADRE! LA CASA ESTA BUENA!

IT SURE IS, AMIGO.

WALDEN SANCTUARY

G B Trudeau

WELCOME. I'M REVEREND SLOAN, AND THIS IS THE WALDEN SANCTUARY.

(PADRE SLOAN WELCOMES YOU TO CASA WALDEN.)

MY SPANISH IS A LITTLE RUSTY, SO SENOR JESÚS GARZA IS HELPING ME OUT TODAY.

(TRANSLATION IS COURTESY OF YOURS TRULY.)

FIRST, A LITTLE HISTORY OF THIS HOUSE, WITH WHICH I HAVE BEEN ASSOCIATED FOR 15 YEARS.

(CASA WALDEN COMES WITH A STORY.)

IN THE BEGINNING, THERE WERE HIPPIES..

(THE ORIGINAL OWNERS USED DRUGS.)

..AND AFTER YOU GET SETTLED IN, I'D LIKE TO SPEAK WITH EACH FAMILY ABOUT YOUR IMMIGRATION STATUS.

(WE'RE GOING TO BE INTERROGATED.)

DESPITE OUR HYPOCRITICAL STATE DEPARTMENT, I THINK YOU'LL FIND THE AMERICAN PEOPLE THEMSELVES TO BE MOST HOSPITABLE!

(HE PREDICTS OPEN ARMS, ETC.)

CONTRARY TO WHAT YOU MAY HAVE CONCLUDED FROM WATCHING EXPORTED U.S. TELEVISION SHOWS..

(REGARDING YOUR IMPRESSIONS BASED ON AMERICAN TV..)

NOT ALL AMERICANS ARE STUPID, RICH OR VIOLENT.

(HE DOESN'T UNDERSTAND "MIAMI VICE.")

G B Trudeau

SO YOU HAVE FAMILY IN NEW YORK. THAT'S GOOD. THAT COULD BE HELPFUL. NOW, WHY DID YOU FLEE TO THE U.S.?

TO ESCAPE POLITICAL REPRESSION IN NICARAGUA.

YOU MEAN, EL SALVADOR. TO ESCAPE REPRESSION IN EL SALVADOR.

NO, NICARAGUA.

>SIGH< THAT'S A PROBLEM. MY FUNDING COMES FROM LIBERATION THEOLOGIANS. NICARAGUA IS SUPPOSED TO BE FREE NOW.

OKAY, EL SALVADOR.

EL SALVADOR, EH? YOU POOR DEVIL!

G B Trudeau

LOOK AT THOSE FACES. ARROGANT TO THE END! WOULDN'T YOU **LOVE** TO KNOW WHAT THE DUVALIERS SPIRITED OUT WITH THEM THE NIGHT THEY FLED?

WELL, YES AND NO..

FRIDAY, FEB

Duvalier Lea

The final drive to the airport. "powerful as a monkey's tail." U.S. of- decided to give up his auth... Baby Doc has l...

SOMETIMES, THE REAL STORY CAN BE..

..UNSPEAKABLY HIDEOUS!

..AND RICK'S ALREADY LEFT TO VISIT HIM IN EXILE. IT'S ONE OF THE FEW INTERVIEWS DUVALIER'S EVER GIVEN!

GOODNESS! THAT **IS** A REMARKABLE ASSIGNMENT!

IT SHOULD YIELD SOME ABSOLUTELY **FASCINATING** INSIGHTS INTO THE GENESIS OF EVIL!

..AND THEN THE OTHER KIDS STARTED CALLING ME "BASKETHEAD."

SO THAT'S WHEN YOU DECIDED TO GET EVEN?

MR. DUVALIER, DO YOU THINK YOUR WIFE'S ILL-TIMED EXTRAVAGANCES CONTRIBUTED TO YOUR FINAL DOWNFALL?

HOW DO YOU MEAN?

WELL, FOR INSTANCE, HER LEAVING FOR A $1.7 MILLION SHOPPING SPREE IN PARIS WHILE HAITI WAS IN THE MIDST OF A SEVERE ECONOMIC CRISIS.

$1.7 MILLION? SHE SPENT $1.7 MILLION IN PARIS?

REPORTEDLY.

WHAT'D SHE DO WITH THE **REST** OF IT!

UM.. I DON'T KNOW. I'D RATHER NOT GET CAUGHT IN THE MIDDLE HERE.

..AND I'M STILL KICKING MYSELF FOR NOT HAVING THEM ALL SHOT!

I SEE.

NO.. NO, THAT DOESN'T SOUND RIGHT. DON'T USE THAT.

UM.. I'M AFRAID WE'RE ON THE RECORD HERE, MR. DUVALIER.

SO WHAT? IT'S **MY** INTERVIEW, AND I JUST TOLD YOU NOT TO USE IT!

IT DOESN'T WORK THAT WAY, SIR. BECAUSE YOU SAID IT ON THE RECORD, I GET TO PRINT IT.

AMAZING.. WHAT'S THAT CALLED?

A FREE PRESS. I COULD SEND YOU SOME LITERATURE ON IT.

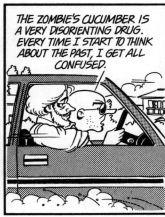

MR. DUPUIS? YES, THIS IS MR. HARRIS. I UNDERSTAND YOU REPRESENT EX-PRESIDENT-FOR-LIFE DUVALIER.

GOOD, GOOD. I'LL TELL YOU WHY I CALLED. I'M VERY INTERESTED IN ACQUIRING ONE OF HIS ZOMBIE SLAVES, A MR. LÉGUME.

WHY? SENTIMENTAL REASONS, MOSTLY. MAY WE NEGOTIATE? GREAT. I'M GOING TO PUT ON MY HIGH-POWERED LEGAL COUNSEL, MS. JOANIE "JAWS" CAUCUS.

"JAWS" HERE.

RING! RING! HEY, **JAWS!** THE ATTORNEY GENERAL ON LINE **TWO!**

HOW FAR DO YOU WANT TO GO WITH THIS?

AS FAR AS WE HAVE TO. I'M A RICH MAN.

MR. DUPUIS? SINCE THE PURCHASE OF HUMAN BEINGS IS FORBIDDEN OUTSIDE OF PRO SPORTS, MY CLIENT HAS ADVISED ME TO OFFER YOU A "FINDER'S FEE" FOR MR. DUKE'S RETURN.

WHAT DO WE HAVE IN MIND? WELL, THAT'S DIFFICULT TO SAY, MR. DUPUIS. HOW CAN WE MEASURE THE VALUE OF A PERSON? IS IT POSSIBLE TO SET A PRICE FOR A HUMAN LIFE?

$10 MILLION. TAKE IT OR LEAVE IT.

PASS. WE'RE NOT TALKING MOTHER TERESA HERE.

.. AND THOSE ARE DUKE'S HEALTH CERTIFICATES. I HAD THEM POUCHED OVER FROM FRANCE.

GOOD THINKING, JOANIE.

LET'S SEE HERE.. HIS WEIGHT IS 145.. THAT'S ABOUT RIGHT. BLOOD PRESSURE IS 20 OVER 30.. GOOD, GOOD..

20 OVER 30 IS **GOOD?**

IT'S NORMAL FOR A ZOMBIE. THEY'RE PRETTY MELLOW. AHA! HIS DENTAL X-RAY! YUP, IT'S DUKE, ALL RIGHT!

HOW CAN YOU TELL?

HIS MOLARS. THAT'S OLD MICROFILM FROM HIS SMUGGLING DAYS.

$4.5 MILLION? THAT DOESN'T WORK FOR US. HOW ABOUT 4.2 ON A 15-YEAR SCHEDULE WITH COLAS? WHAT? NO.. THAT WON'T DO..

WE'RE WASTING VALUABLE TIME HERE, COUNSELOR. LET ME GIVE IT A SHOT..

UM.. MR. DUPUIS, MY CLIENT WOULD LIKE TO TALK TO YOU PERSONALLY..

DUPUIS? HARRIS HERE! THIS ISN'T AN ARAB BAZAAR, MON AMI! ALL I'VE GOT IS $17 MIL CASH! TAKE IT OR LEAVE IT!

DONE. SEE, YOU JUST HAVE TO BE FORCEFUL.

OH, ZONKER..

Panel 1: WE'RE BACK, CAMPERS. MY PRODUCER JAKE AND I WERE JUST TALKING ABOUT THE LATEST ADMINISTRATION SCANDAL, THIS ONE INVOLVING CIVIL RIGHTS CHIEF CLARENCE PENDLETON.

Panel 2: IT REMINDED ME THAT IT'S ABOUT TIME FOR AN UPDATE OF OUR RUNNING TALLY OF REAGAN APPOINTEES CHARGED WITH LEGAL OR ETHICAL MISCONDUCT.

Panel 3: SO HERE IT IS, THE DEFINITIVE LIST OF BACK-SCRATCHERS, TILL-DIPPERS, AND CONSCIENCE-CUTTERS, THE UNABRIDGED 1986 "SLEAZE ON PARADE"! UH-OH...

Panel 4: LET'S WADE IN UP TO OUR ARMPITS, SHALL WE? SWITCH TO 5-SECOND DELAY!

Panel 5: YES, IT'S TIME FOR "SLEAZE ON PARADE"! LET'S START WITH REAGAN APPOINTEES WHO RESIGNED OR WERE FIRED FOLLOWING CHARGES OF LEGAL OR ETHICAL MISCONDUCT!

Panel 6: HERE WE GO..."RITA LAVELLE, JOSEPH CANZERI, LOUIS CORDIA, MICHAEL CARDENAS, WESLEY A. PLUMMER, MARY ANN GILLEECE, FRED J. VILLELLA, LOUIS O. GIUFFRIDA..."

Panel 7: "...JAMES WATT, MICHAEL CONNOLLY, ROBERT FUNKHOUSER, ROBERT NIMMO, THOMAS C. REED! ARMAND REISER! EMANUEL SAVAS! CARLOS CAMPBELL! PETER BIBKO!"

Panel 8: WHOA. BETTER PACE MYSELF... WANT ME TO TAKE A SHIFT?

Panel 9: ...AND CONTINUING WITH REAGAN OFFICIALS WHO LEFT OFFICE AMIDST CHARGES OF UNETHICAL BEHAVIOR OR CRIMINAL WRONGDOING...

Panel 10: "RAYMOND P. DONOVAN, ANNE BURFORD, JAMES M. BEGGS, JOHN McELDERRY, DONALD I. HOVDE, MICHAEL KAREM, JOHN HORTON..."

Panel 11: "...JOHN HERNANDEZ, JAMES R. HARRIS, SHELBY BREWER, GUY W. FISKE, JOHN FEDDERS, MATTHEW N. NOVICK, RICHARD MULBERRY, AND ROBERT M. PERRY!"

Panel 12: WHEW! I THOUGHT HE'D NEVER... PAGE TWO.

Panel 13: "...AND FROM OUR SLEAZE GRAB BAG, MICHAEL DEAVER, WILLIAM J. CASEY, MICHAEL FROST, GERALD P. CARMEN, ROBERT BURFORD, EDGAR CALLAHAN, AND CHARLES Z. WICK."

Panel 14: OKAY, BEFORE WE CONTINUE WITH THIS SORDID LITTLE EXERCISE, IT PROBABLY BEHOOVES US TO STOP AND QUESTION THE BASIC FAIRNESS OF A ROLL-CALL OF SHAME.

Panel 15: IS IT FAIR TO SIMPLY READ A LIST OF NAMES COLD? ARE YOU GETTING THE WHOLE STORY HERE? WELL, IN ALL CANDOR, PROBABLY NOT.

Panel 16: SO REMEMBER, THESE ARE JUST THE GUYS WHO GOT CAUGHT...

"... DONALD ELLISON, EMBEZZLED BANK FUNDS, IMPRISONED. LEE S. VARNER, DEFRAUDED FEDERAL GOVERNMENT OF $53,500, CONVICTED..."

Hi! Remember me? I'm your boss.

"RICHARD V. ALLEN, ACCEPTED MONEY AND WATCHES, RESIGNED..."

Both of us work for National Public Radio.

Our budget is approved by The White House.

"ED MEESE, AIDED FINANCIALLY BY SIX PERSONS LATER GIVEN FEDERAL JOBS, PROMOTED."

AVOID THE RUSH, FOLKS! CLEAN OUT YOUR DESKS NOW!

...get is ...d by

GOOD NEWS, BOYS AND GIRLS! HERE ON THE LINE WITH AN OPPOSING VIEWPOINT IS WHITE HOUSE SPOKESMAN LARRY SPEAKES! SPEAK TO US, SPEAKES!

"NPR'S SO-CALLED 'SLEAZE ON PARADE' IS AN OUTRAGE. THE 103 APPOINTEES NAMED ARE **ALL** VICTIMS OF VICIOUS SMEAR CAMPAIGNS BY THE LIBERAL PRESS."

"THE PRESIDENT HAS TOTAL CONFIDENCE IN THE INNOCENCE AND INTEGRITY OF EVERY INDIVIDUAL LISTED..."

NOT GONNA GIVE AN INCH, EH?

..."WITH THE POSSIBLE EXCEPTION OF THOSE BEHIND BARS."

THERE! WAS THAT SO HARD?

IT WAS 3:45 A.M. WHEN THE NIGHT PORTER SIGNED FOR THE CRATE FROM MARSEILLES...

M. Zonker Harris
Baby Doc Group
Port-au-
HAITI

SAR? SAR?

HUNKLE DOOOKE?

SIR? CAN YOU HEAR ME?

HE DOESN'T LOOK SO GOOD...

SIR? DO YOU REMEMBER ME? DEAN HONEY?

NO... I CAN'T... I... ≶ COUGH! ≶

I'LL BE RIGHT BACK.

TAKE IT EASY, BIG GUY.

WHAT'S GOING ON? WHERE... WHERE... AM I?

YOU'RE BACK AT THE COLLEGE. YOU'VE BEEN UNDER THE INFLUENCE OF A ZOMBIE COMPOUND. WE'RE GOING TO TRY TO DRY YOU OUT. SO JUST RELAX, OKAY?

REMEMBER NOW, SIR?

HONEY! YOU'LL FRIGHTEN HIM!

AAAG..

UM... HONEY, I THINK WE MIGHT BE OVERLOADING UNCLE DUKE'S CIRCUITS A LITTLE HERE. MAYBE IF I COULD BE ALONE WITH HIM...

YOU? BUT YOU DON'T HAVE THE SAME INTIMATE RAPPORT THAT...

WHAT ARE YOU TALKING ABOUT? I'VE KNOWN UNCLE DUKE MOST OF MY LIFE!

MAYBE, BUT I'M HIS SECOND-IN-COMMAND HERE, AND I...

HONEY, I PAID FOR HIM!

THAT'S IT, LORD IT OVER ME!

I DON'T TRUST THIS CHICK. SHE'S GOT PATERNITY SUIT WRITTEN ALL OVER HER.

ANY PROGRESS?

NAW. HE'S STILL PRETTY OUT OF IT.

HE'S BEEN ON THAT ZOMBIE PASTE FOR WEEKS, THOUGH. IT'LL PROBABLY BE SOME TIME BEFORE HE REALLY SHAKES IT.

WHAT HE REALLY NEEDS NOW IS A GOOD NIGHT OF Z'S. I JUST LEFT STRICT ORDERS HE ISN'T TO BE DISTURBED!

TRY TO REMEMBER, SIR! WE WERE DEEPLY IN LOVE!

DON'T YOU EVER KNOCK?

NOT THAT I RE-GRET IT, BUT IT SURE IS WEIRD BLOWING $17 MILLION IN ONE DAY...

I GUESS IT'S BACK TO CLIPPING COUPONS AND IRONING MY OWN T-SHIRTS. ALL I'VE GOT LEFT NOW IS MY MEMORIES.

AND YOUR MONET, OF COURSE.

OH, RIGHT. HEY, HOW DO YOU THINK IT LOOKS OVER THE MINI-BAR?

ITEM: NANCY REAGAN'S INAUGURAL BALL GOWN, ON DISPLAY AT THE SMITH-SONIAN, IS STRETCHING AT THE RATE OF HALF AN INCH A YEAR!

MUSEUM OFFICIALS SAY IT WILL COST $10,000 TO "STABILIZE" THE HAND-BEADED, WHITE SATIN SHEATH. BUT INCREDIBLY, THE FUNDS ARE NOT AVAILABLE!

A NATION THAT IS UNABLE TO CHECK THE GROWTH OF A FIRST LADY'S GOWN IS A NATION IN SHAME. JOIN US AS WE EXAMINE THE TRAGIC COST OF A MINDLESS BUDGETARY MECHANISM IN...

Guaranteed True!

GRAMM-RUDMAN

HORROR STORIES!

FIRST IN A SERIES...

THE UNCHECKED STRETCHING OF NANCY REAGAN'S INAUGURAL GOWN. AN INCREDIBLE BUT TRUE GRAMM-RUDMAN *HORROR STORY!*

HERE AT THE SMITHSONIAN'S MUSEUM OF AMERICAN HISTORY, OFFICIALS SAY THE SATIN GALANOS CREATION HAS ALREADY GROWN 2"! BUT THE $10,000 NEEDED TO "STABILIZE" THE GOWN HAS BEEN CUT!

WHAT ARE THE CONSEQUENCES? USING AN ANIMATION SIMULATOR, WE CAN PROJECT WHAT THE GROWING GOWN WILL LOOK LIKE TO A MUSEUM VISITOR IN THE YEAR 2050.

WHETHER HISTORY WILL FORGIVE US REMAINS TO BE SEEN.

MUSEUM ADMINISTRATOR BABS CRYER TALKS OPENLY ABOUT THE BUDGETARY NIGHTMARE THAT HAS LEFT MRS. REAGAN'S GOWN TWISTING IN THE WIND.

FRANKLY, WE'RE IN A STATE. SINCE STAFF SALARIES ARE FIXED COSTS, GRAMM-RUDMAN MEANS WE'LL HAVE TO CUT ALL PROGRAMS AND IMPROVEMENTS BY HALF!

SO YOUR HOPE IS THAT NEWS OF THE GOWN'S CONDITION WILL GENERATE SUPPORT IN CERTAIN QUARTERS? WHAT-EVER DO YOU MEAN?

UH...MOMMY... WE'RE IN A SECURITY BRIEFING... THIS IS AN *EMERGENCY!*

AS THE SATIN SHEATH WITH THE FERN MOTIF AND EMBROIDERED CRYSTAL BEADS INCHES, INEXORABLY, DOWNWARD, A NATION'S PRIDE HANGS BY A THREAD!

WHAT CAN *YOU* DO? WELL, START BY GETTING INVOLVED!

SHOW YOU CARE BY SENDING YOUR TAX-DEDUCTIBLE CONTRIBUTION TO...

"SAVE THE GOWN" c/o NATIONAL MUSEUM of AMERICAN HISTORY 14TH AND CONSTITUTION AVENUE, N.W. WASH., D.C. 20560

TOMORROW: KIDS! HOW *YOU* CAN HELP!

KIDS! YOU, TOO, CAN HELP IN THE CAMPAIGN TO STABILIZE THE FIRST LADY'S GOWN! HERE ARE SOME IDEAS!

"SELL MAGAZINE SUBSCRIPTIONS..." ...AND 34 WEEKS OF "LIFE" PAYS FOR THE RESTORATION OF THREE BEADS! COUNT US IN, BILLY!

"...OR STAGE YOUR OWN BENEFIT INAUGURAL PAGEANT!" DA, DA, DA, DA, DA, DUM!

BUT, REMEMBER, KIDS! *DON'T* KEEP THE MONEY FOR YOURSELVES! SEND IT TO... THE NATIONAL MUSEUM OF AMERICAN HISTORY, 14TH AND CONSTITUTION AVE., N.W., WASH., D.C., *20560!*

PART

THREE

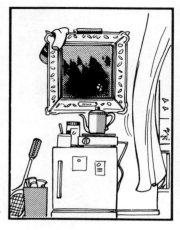

CURTIS! THERE'S MAYONNAISE ON MY MONET!

I TOLD YOU THAT WASN'T A GOOD PLACE TO HANG IT, MAN!

SAVE THE GOWN! To make a pledge call (202) 357-4025

SO HOW'D THE MAYONNAISE GET ON MY MONET, CURTIS?

WHAT'S THE BIG DEAL, DUDE? IT'LL WASH OFF.

CURTIS, THAT PAINTING IS WORTH OVER $3 MILLION.

SO SELL IT! YOU WOULDN'T ALWAYS BE HITTING ME UP FOR MONEY!

YOU THINK YOU'D BE PROUD TO BE LIVING WITH A MASTERPIECE.

FRANKLY, MAN, IT DOESN'T LOOK AS GOOD AS WHAT WAS THERE BEFORE.

IT DOESN'T LOOK AS GOOD AS A BEER CAN PYRAMID?

THE PYRAMID WAS A MORE HONEST STATE- MENT, MAN.

I GOTTA TELL YOU, DUDE, THIS BUSI- NESS OF OWNING A $3 MILLION PAINT- ING AND BEING DEAD BROKE IS WARPED!

WHAT DO YOU THINK I SHOULD DO?

SELL IT, MAN! USE THE MONEY FOR SOMETHING THAT'LL MAKE A DIFFERENCE!

LIKE WHAT?

I DUNNO. SOME- THING THAT WON'T JUST SIT IN YOUR ROOM. SOMETHING THAT WILL BENE- FIT MANKIND!

YOU MEAN, LIKE A HOCKEY TEAM OR SOMETHING?

THERE YOU GO.

WHAT'S THAT, CURTIS?

AN ALTERNATIVE TO MONET. THE 1986 PEERAGE LISTINGS!

HUH?

BRITISH TITLES THAT ARE ON THE MARKET! FOR $17,000 TO $75,000, YOU CAN BUY A LORD- SHIP! ALL YOU GOTTA DO IS PASS AN INTER- VIEW!

WHERE'D YOU GET THIS?

FOUND IT WHEN I WAS CLEARING OUT DUKE'S PERSONAL PAPERS. APPARENTLY, HE WAS THINKING OF BECOMING AN EARL OR DUKE!

DUKE DUKE?

OR THE EARL OF DUKE! IS THAT TOTALLY RAD OR WHAT?

COMMANDER LESS-THAN-ZERO, PLEASE TELL THIS COMMITTEE...

EXCUSE ME, SEÑORA, BUT MY NEW NOM DE GUERRE IS "COMMANDER NATHAN HALE."

VERY WELL, MR. HALE. PLEASE TELL THIS COMMITTEE TO WHAT EXTENT YOU AND YOUR MEN ARE CONTROLLED BY THE CONTRA DIRECTORATE.

WHO?

THE DIRECTORATE. THE NICARAGUANS APPOINTED BY THE CIA TO REPRESENT YOUR POLITICAL INTERESTS.

OH, YOU MEAN THE NERDS!

YOUR CIVILIAN LEADERS ARE NERDS?

NO OFFENSE, BUT WHERE'D YOU FIND THOSE PEOPLE?

COMMANDER, IF YOU CAN'T ACCOUNT FOR MUCH OF THE $27 MILLION WE SENT YOU LAST YEAR, WHY SHOULD CONGRESS HAND YOU ANOTHER $100 MILLION?

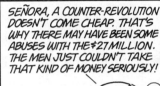

SEÑORA, A COUNTER-REVOLUTION DOESN'T COME CHEAP. THAT'S WHY THERE MAY HAVE BEEN SOME ABUSES WITH THE $27 MILLION. THE MEN JUST COULDN'T TAKE THAT KIND OF MONEY SERIOUSLY!

$100 MILLION, ON THE OTHER HAND, TELLS THE FREEDOM FIGHTER THAT YOU VALUE AND RESPECT THE JOB HE'S DOING! IT TELLS HIM YOU **TRUST** HIM WITH MEANINGFUL AMOUNTS OF AID!

BUT WE DON'T.

FINE. THEN **YOU** TELL THAT TO THE MEN AT BASE CAMP "VALLEY FORGE".

THAT'S GREAT, TRIP-MAN. I'M THRILLED TO PIECES FOR YOU. HAVE A GOOD ONE.

YOUR ROOMMATE GOT A SUMMER JOB, DEAR?

DON'T START ON ME, MOM.

I'M JUST CURIOUS, THAT'S ALL.

HE GOT SOME KIND OF INTERNSHIP WITH A COLUMNIST NAMED GEORGE WILL, OKAY?

T. HAMILTON TRIPLER TO SEE DR. WILL.

AH, YES, THE NEW QUOTE BOY!

T. HAMILTON TRIPLER, SIR. THE NEW QUOTE BOY!

WELCOME TO OUR SHOP, TRIPLER. I'M HIGGINS, QUOTE SUPERVISOR.

I ASSUME YOU'RE FAMILIAR WITH OUR END OF THINGS. WE PROVIDE THE FLOURISHES OF ERUDITION SO INDISPENSABLE TO A GEORGE WILL COMMENTARY.

IT'S NOT AS SIMPLE AS IT SOUNDS. THE EFFORTLESS RECALL OF EXQUISITELY GERMANE SAYINGS IS A LOST ART. YOUR PREDECESSOR WAS A CASE IN POINT.

IS IT TRUE HE WAS FIRED FOR QUOTING ROCK LYRICS?

THERE WAS SOME UNPLEASANTNESS, YES.

...AND OVER THERE ARE DEBATE RECORDS FROM THE SCOTTISH PARLIAMENT BEFORE IT WAS DISSOLVED IN 1707. REMEMBER, KEEP YOUR REFERENCES OBSCURE!

DR. WILL THINKS OUR CULTURE IS IN A SHAMEFUL STATE, SO AVOID QUOTING THE MODERNS. STICK WITH ARCANE TORY PHILOSOPHERS OR THEIR CONTEMPORARIES.

SHAKESPEARE IS DEPENDABLE, BUT ONLY QUOTE THE EARLY FOLIOS. THE HAPSBURGS ARE FINE, AS ARE PAST PRESIDENTS OF PRINCETON AND, OF COURSE, PROFESSIONAL BASEBALL PLAYERS.

BASEBALL PLAYERS?

DR. WILL'S LINK TO THE COMMON MAN. BUT KEEP THEM SHORT.

QUOTE BOY! I NEED SOMETHING ON THE BANALITY OF CONTEMPORARY SOCIETY!

RIGHT AWAY, DR. WILL!

THWIP! THWIIP! THWIP!

THWIP!

WELL?

UH... UH...

THWIP! THWIP!

"DON'T YOU JUST HATE PAPERCLIPS? I KNOW I DO."—ANDY ROONEY.

WELL?

...AND I WANT A QUOTE FROM "BLEAK HOUSE" FOR MONDAY, AND SOME BON MOTS FROM TWAIN FOR MY SPEECH TO THE REALTORS.

YES, SIR, DR. WILL.

ON TUESDAY'S COLUMN, THE SECOND GRAPH SEEMS A LITTLE BARREN. LET'S BE PUCKISH AND DROP IN SOMETHING GAULISH, IN THE ORIGINAL FRENCH.

TRY VOLTAIRE OR PERHAPS ROUSSEAU, OR THE PROGRAM NOTES AT LA COMÉDIE-FRANÇAISE.

SHALL WE PROVIDE A TRANSLATION FOR YOUR SLOWER READERS, SIR?

NON. CE N'EST PAS NÉCESSAIRE.

TRÈS BIEN.

IF GARY HART'S DEMEANOR ONCE EVOKED PASSAGES FROM THE HINDU EPIC, BHAGAVADGITA, TODAY HE PROVIDES GRAY REMINDERS OF BISHOP LAUD'S ADVICE TO CHARLES I.

WE ARE THE LESS WELL-HEELED FOR IT. ONE CAN ALMOST TASTE, ON THE MIND'S PALATE, THE PUNGENCY OF GÖTTERDÄMMERUNG, BRAISED IN THE JUICES OF THE WAGNERIAN ZEITGEIST.

WHAT REMAINS IS MUNDANE. AS PIET MONDRIAN IS SAID TO HAVE SCRIBBLED IN THE MARGINS OF A MONOGRAPH LATER PUBLISHED IN DE STIJL, "PICK UP LAUNDRY, MILK".

HE USED IT!

DON'T GET COCKY.

"HERE, THATCHER, TAKING A PAGE FROM DE GAULLE, THROWS THE BOOK AT TALLEYRAND'S DICTUM, 'SURTOUT PAS TROP DE ZÈLE.'"

"HOW DISTANT SEEM THE CROWDS WHO ONCE GREETED POPE URBAN IV WITH CRIES OF 'DEUS ES! DEUS ES!' HOW FAINT SEEMS LORD BYRON'S LAMENT IN CANTO II OF DON JUAN."

WOW... THE BOSS IS REALLY IN TOP FORM THESE DAYS, ISN'T HE?

YEAH, BUT SOMETIMES I HAVE TO WONDER WHO READS THE STUFF. AND WHY.

HERE'S ONE FROM BYRON YOU CAN USE AT THE WEDDING...

"DEUS ES," YOUR MAJESTY!

HI, THIS IS YOUR WINDOW SEAT, ISN'T IT? I'M AFRAID I GRABBED IT. YOU DON'T MIND, DO YOU? I CAN MOVE.

UH... NO, NO, THAT'S OKAY.

THANKS, YOU'RE A DREAMBOAT. SO WHAT'S YOUR NAME? MINE'S MARCIA FEINBLOOM.

I'M ZONKER, VISCOUNT ST. AUSTELL-IN-THE-MOOR BIGGLESWADE-BRIXHAM.

WHOA. OKAY, I'M IMPRESSED.

THANK YOU.

MAY I JUST CALL YOU ZONKER?

I'M AFRAID NOT. SORRY.

SO ARE YOU GOING TO THE ROYAL WEDDING, VISCOUNT ST. WHATCHAMA-CALLIT?

ST. AUSTELL-IN-THE-MOOR BIGGLESWADE-BRIXHAM. YES, I AM.

YOU MUST BE THRILLED! WHERE ARE THEY HAVING IT?

WESTMINSTER ABBEY. A RETURN TO THE TRADITION SET BY HENRY I WITH HIS MARRIAGE TO MATILDA OF SCOTLAND IN 1100.

PRINCE ANDREW'S WILL BE THE 14TH ROYAL WEDDING HELD IN THE ABBEY. THERE'VE ALSO BEEN 37 CORONATIONS, BEGINNING WITH WILLIAM THE CONQUEROR'S IN 1066.

BOY... YOU KNOW YOUR STUFF!

THANK YOU. WANT TO HEAR A QUOTE FROM GEORGE WILL?

SO HOW'D YOU GET INVITED TO THE WEDDING, VISCOUNT? DO ALL YOU NOBLES GET TO GO?

NO. THE LORD CHAMBERLAIN DRAWS UP AN EXCLUSIVE LIST.

APPARENTLY, MY PREDECESSOR WAS A COURT FAVORITE. HE TRANSFERRED HIS INVITATION TO ME WHEN I ACQUIRED HIS TITLE.

ACQUIRED IT? YOU MEAN YOU WEREN'T BORN A VISCOUNT?

NO, I WAS BORN A SURFER. EVERYTHING I KNOW ABOUT ROYALS, I PICKED UP FROM "DEBRETT'S."

INCREDIBLE! AND THE ENGLISH ACCENT?

MONTY PYTHON RECORDS.

Panel 1: THIS IS ROLAND HEDLEY. TODAY THE CIA STEPPED OUT INTO THE WARM SUNSHINE OF **OVERT** OPERATIONS.

Panel 2: AT ANDREWS AIR FORCE BASE, TOP "COMPANY" OPERATIVES LEFT ON THEIR MISSION TO DIRECT THE WAR AGAINST NICARAGUA'S SANDINISTAS.

Panel 3: FINALLY FREED FROM THE NEED TO KEEP CIA INVOLVEMENT SECRET, SPOOK SPOUSES TURNED OUT IN DROVES FOR FAREWELL CEREMONIES.

Make them say Uncle, dear!

GIVE 'EM HECK, HONEY!

Panel 4: SUSAN, HAS YOUR HUSBAND TOLD YOU HIS CODE NAME?

YES, IT'S "REX." ISN'T THAT THE CUTEST?

©B Trudeau

Panel 5: HERE'S YOUR BOURBON, MR...

BLACKBURN, HONEY! TERRY BLACKBURN, JR! CODE NAME, "HAVOC"!

Panel 6: THAT'S A CUTE CODE NAME, HAVOC. WHAT TAKES YOU GUYS TO TEGUCIGALPA? BUSINESS?

NOPE. GUESS AGAIN, SWEET THANG.

Panel 7: GIVE ME A TEENY HINT.

OKAY. IT HAS TO DO WITH PRESERVING FREEDOM AND DEMOCRATIC INSTITUTIONS.

Panel 8: MY **GOD!** YOU'RE THE GUYS WHO ARE GOING TO OVERTHROW THAT GOVERNMENT!

YOU TOLD HER!

HELL, HAVOC, IT'S RIGHT HERE IN "USA TODAY."

©B Trudeau

Panel 9: EXCUSE ME, SEÑOR, HAVE YOU SEEN MY COUSIN MARCOS?

YOU'RE LOOKIN' AT HIM, AMIGO! THANKS FOR MEETING ME.

Panel 10: THEY SAY THE DOG BAYS IN CHICAGO.

YOU CAN SKIP THE CLOAK-AND-K-BAR, JACK. WE'RE OUT OF THE CLOSET NOW. WE CAN BOOGIE IN PUBLIC!

Panel 11: (no dialogue)

Panel 12: THEY SAY THE DOG BAYS IN CHICAGO.

ONLY WHEN THE FAT MAN DOES HIS LAUNDRY. SATISFIED?

©B Trudeau

Panel 13: COMANDANTE LESS-THAN-ZERO IS ANXIOUS TO SEE YOU, SIR. ALL OF TEGUCIGALPA IS ABUZZ OVER THE $100 MILLION IN CONTRA AID!

Panel 14: AH, TEGUCIGALPA! THE BIG GOOSE! SHE SURE HAS CHANGED SINCE WE FIRST SET UP SHOP HERE!

Panel 15: GO, CIA!

Panel 16: STILL HAS THAT SMALL TOWN FEEL, THOUGH, DOESN'T IT?

AS I SAY, EVERYONE'S EXCITED ABOUT THE MONEY.

©B Trudeau

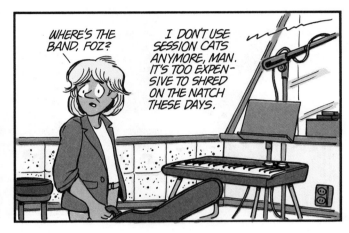

114.

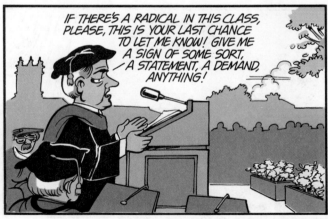

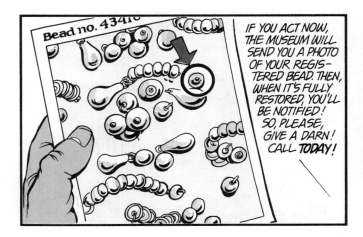

... AND THE CIA WANTS US IN WASHINGTON FOR A MEETING ON TUESDAY.

YOU'LL HAVE TO GO WITHOUT ME, AMIGO. I'VE ALREADY GOT A DRUG PICKUP PENCILED IN.

OKAY, SO MUCH FOR THE DRUG-SMUGGLING OPERATION. LET'S MOVE ON TO THE CONGRESSIONAL INVESTIGATION OF MISSING CONTRA FUNDS. JORGE?

NOTHING MUCH TO REPORT, COMANDANTE. THE G.A.O. HAS ABOUT GIVEN UP ON TRYING TO FIGURE OUT WHAT WE DID WITH THE MONEY.

WHAT ABOUT THE NEXT $100 MILLION? CAN WE ABSORB IT?

IF WE USE MORE MIDDLEMEN AND OFFSHORE BANKS, NO PROBLEM.

WHAT ABOUT THE PAYOFFS TO THE HONDURAN MILITARY?

I DON'T THINK THAT SHOULD COME OUT OF OUR POCKETS ANYMORE. LET THE CIA EXPENSE-ACCOUNT IT.

HEAR, HEAR. THEY'RE THE ONES WHO LEASED HONDURAS IN THE FIRST PLACE.

OKAY, I THINK THAT TAKES CARE OF OLD AND NEW BUSINESS... CAN ANYONE THINK OF ANYTHING ELSE?

FREEDOM-FIGHTING?

OH, RIGHT... BATTLEFIELD REPORT!

LET'S SEE... I THINK WE BLEW UP A CLINIC.

©B Trudeau

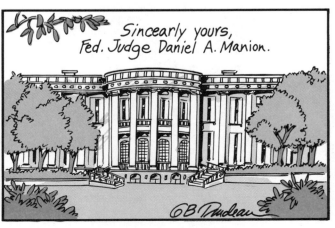

SORRY, MATTY. RICK'S NOT HOME...

HE WENT DOWN TO THE PAT ROBERTSON PRESS CONFERENCE.

PAT ROBERTSON? NO KIDDING?

UH-HUH. RICK'S GOT A LITTLE PROBLEM HE'S HOPING ROBERTSON CAN HELP HIM WITH.

JESUS, **DRIVE** THE HICCUPS FROM THIS REPORTER!

HEY... THEY'RE GONE!

SIR? DO YOU DO HEMORRHOIDS, TOO?

IF THERE ARE NO MORE HANGNAILS AND HERNIAS TO HEAL, I HAVE JOYFUL NEWS FOR YOU ALL TODAY!

IT HAS FINALLY COME TO PASS. THE LORD GOD HAS PERSONALLY ASKED ME TO CONSIDER RUNNING FOR PRESIDENT!

HE HAS BESEECHED ME TO ANNOUNCE A PAT ROBERTSON EXPLORATORY CANDIDACY, A CRUSADE WITH THE HOLY BLESSING OF GOD ALMIGHTY AND OUR SAVIOUR, JESUS OF NAZARETH.

BEATS AN ENDORSEMENT FROM THE TEAMSTERS

SHH!

GOD HAS ALSO ASKED ME TO SET UP A NEW TOLL-FREE NUMBER...

...AND GOD CAME TO ME IN THE NIGHT, AND AFTER WE HAD EXCHANGED PLEASANTRIES, HE SAID, "PAT, IT'S TIME TO CRYSTALLIZE YOUR DECISION."

HIS COMMENT, HOWEVER, WAS NOT FOR ATTRIBUTION. GOD WAS SPEAKING ON BACKGROUND.

UM...WHOM SHOULD WE SOURCE IT TO, THEN, SIR?

CELESTIAL INSIDERS.

"CELESTIAL INSIDERS"?

GOD DOESN'T WANT TO APPEAR TO BE TAKING SIDES.

MR. ROBERTSON, WHEN DID YOU FINALLY GET THE GO-AHEAD FOR THIS EXPLORATORY EFFORT?

WELL, GOD AND I TALKED SEVERAL TIMES WHEN I WAS BACK IN VIRGINIA BEACH LAST WEEK. WE WENT OVER THE MICHIGAN RESULTS IN SOME DETAIL.

I THINK IT WAS THURSDAY WHEN I RECEIVED THE FINAL WORD.

AND WHAT **WAS** THAT WORD, EXACTLY?

I DON'T KNOW HOW TO SAY IT IN ENGLISH. WE SPEAK IN TONGUES.

COULD YOU SPELL IT PHONETICALLY? WE CAN GET IT TRANSLATED.

Panel 1: MR. ROBERTSON, THERE ARE MILLIONS OF AMERICANS WHO, FRANKLY, ARE MADE A LITTLE NERVOUS BY A MAN WHO HAS DETAILED, PRIVATE CONVERSATIONS WITH GOD.

Panel 2: DO YOU THINK YOU CAN OVERCOME... / WHAT'S THAT?

Panel 3: I SAID... / I'M NOT TALKING TO YOU.

Panel 4: OH. BETTER SIT DOWN. SLOWLY. / YOU SAY THE PRESS CONFERENCE IS OVER? THY WILL BE DONE.

Panel 5: REVEREND, IN THE PAST, YOU HAVE ADVOCATED THE KILLING OF GADHAFI, THE BANNING OF HALLOWEEN, AND FORGIVING THE NATIONAL DEBT EVERY 50 YEARS.

Panel 6: WHAT'S YOUR REACTION TO THE WIDESPREAD SNICKERING IN THE PRESS OVER THESE PROPOSALS? / WELL, I CERTAINLY DON'T BLAME THE REPORTERS.

Panel 7: MOST REPORTERS ARE SIMPLY DOING THEIR JOBS. IT'S THEIR SECULAR HUMANIST MASTERS, THE EDITORS, WHO ARE FORCES FOR EVIL, SATANS IN EYE-SHADES!

Panel 8: NO ARGUMENT HERE. / GOT *THAT* RIGHT. / THIS GUY'S OKAY.

Panel 9: I'M GOING TO HATE IT. / YOU DON'T KNOW THAT, MIKE.

Panel 10: YES, I DO. THIS WAS A *VERY* BIG MISTAKE! / HEY, C'MON, GIVE IT A CHANCE, WILLYA?

Panel 11: WHAT HAVE I *DONE?* / OKAY, FINISHED. TAKE A LOOK!

Panel 12: AAIEEE! / WELCOME TO THE '80s, GOOD-LOOKIN'!

Panel 13: YOU DON'T LIKE IT? / J.J., I WANTED A *TRIM!* YOU'VE MADE ME LOOK LIKE SOME JERKY, DOWNTOWN TRENDOID!

Panel 14: MY TRANSFORMATION INTO DORK OF THE YEAR IS NOW COMPLETE! YOU HAVE OFFICIALLY TAKEN OVER MY ENTIRE LIFE!

Panel 15: MIKE, LET'S TALK. SIT DOWN... / ON WHAT? OUR SO-CALLED FURNITURE? / IF YOU INSIST!

Panel 16: MIKE, I... / *WELL?* AREN'T YOU GOING TO WRAP ME UP IN PLASTIC FIRST?

...AND IN THE SPIRIT OF FULL DISCLOSURE, I WILL ALSO MAKE MY CHEST X-RAYS AVAILABLE!

THIS SILLY MAN IS MY OPPONENT?

IN THIS TIME OF NATIONAL CRISIS, THOSE WHO SEEK PUBLIC OFFICE HAVE A SPECIAL OBLIGATION TO SET AN EXAMPLE!

I THEREFORE CHALLENGE MY OPPONENT TO MEET ME, IN ANY VENUE, TO CERTIFY THAT EACH OF US IS DRUG-FREE!

DRUG-FREE? WHAT ON EARTH IS GOING ON HERE?

I BELIEVE THE CAMPAIGN JUST TURNED INTO A P---ING MATCH.

A WHAT? I CAN'T UNDERSTAND WHEN YOU USE HYPHENS, DEAR.

WHY HASN'T MY OPPONENT TAKEN AS FORCEFUL A POSITION ON DRUGS? WHAT MAY WE INFER FROM THAT?

THAT SHE ISN'T AS AGAINST DRUGS AS YOU ARE?

I JUST HEARD THAT MRS. DAVENPORT ISN'T AGAINST DRUGS!

GOOD LORD! SHE ACTUALLY FAVORS THEM?

THE WORD IS THAT DAVENPORT LIKES DRUGS!

WELL, I ALWAYS SUSPECTED SHE USED THEM.

...AND PERSISTENT REPORTS SUGGEST MRS. DAVENPORT HAS A SERIOUS DRUG DEPENDENCY!

IS OUR CURRENT REPRESENTATIVE DRUG-FREE? UNLIKE HER CHALLENGER, MRS. DAVENPORT SAYS IT'S NONE OF OUR BUSINESS.

WHAT'S LACEY DAVENPORT HIDING? THE FOLLOWING VIDEOTAPE SUGGESTS ONE POSSIBLE EXPLANATION.

THIS IS OUR CONGRESSWOMAN IN A COMMITTEE HEARING LAST SUMMER, CLEARLY "NODDING OFF" DURING TESTIMONY!

THAT'S SOUTH OF THE SUSPENDERS, MISTER!

GEORGE SHULTZ WAS TESTIFYING, FOR HEAVEN'S SAKE!

WE STILL HAVE A PROBLEM, BOSS.

...AND HERE AGAIN, MRS. DAVENPORT IS CLEARLY "NODDING OFF.".

DAMAGE CONTROL TIME. I'LL CALL MIKE AT THE AGENCY.

I'LL HAVE HIM PULL TOGETHER SOME FAST TV SPOTS TO COUNTER CLYDE'S INNUENDOS.

IS THAT REALLY NECESSARY, DEAR?

LACEY, CLYDE'S THROWING THEM LOW AND HARD. WE HAVE TO GO ON THE OFFENSIVE BEFORE IT GETS OUT OF CONTROL.

WOULDN'T IT BE BETTER TO JUST IGNORE HIM?

IS LACEY DAVENPORT A JUNKIE?...

TRUST ME.

OKAY, WE OPEN WITH A KIND OF SCRAPBOOK, UNDERSCORING YOUR STRAIGHT-LACED, VICTORIAN UPBRINGING, ETC...

V.O. Back in 1912...

THEN THE VOICE-OVER SAYS, "SHE TOOK HER FIRST AND LAST PILL UPON HEARING ABOUT THE OUTBREAK OF WORLD WAR II. THAT PILL WAS AN ASPIRIN."

...THEN THE ANNOUNCER DROPS HIS VOICE A LITTLE AND INTONES, "DAVENPORT. CLEAN SINCE 1939." FADE OUT. LIKE IT?

DAVENPORT. Clean Since 1939.
V.O.

IT MAKES IT SOUND LIKE I DIDN'T TAKE A BATH DURING THE DEPRESSION.

HMM... COULD YOU SOFTEN IT A LITTLE, MIKE?

YOU DON'T LIKE "DAVENPORT. CLEAN SINCE 1939"?

IT MAKES IT SOUND LIKE THE ISSUE IS HYGIENE. THIS WHOLE DEBATE IS SO UNDIGNIFIED!

I AGREE, MA'AM, BUT LIKE IT OR NOT, THE AGENDA'S BEEN SET. YOU'VE GOT TO PUT THE DRUG ISSUE TO REST.

MICHAEL'S RIGHT, LACEY.

I DISAGREE. I THINK STOOPING TO CONQUER IS DISGRACEFUL. IT'S NOT THE WAY I WAS BROUGHT UP!

HOW ABOUT, "DAVENPORT. NOT EVEN TRACE AMOUNTS."

I'VE GOT TO RUN. PAY THIS NICE BOY FOR HIS TIME, WILL YOU, DEAR?

LACEY DAVENPORT, FOR TEN YEARS, INTERESTED IN YOU AS A PERSON.

SHE'S TIDY. A STICKLER FOR DETAIL. SHE BROOKS NO UNPLEASANTNESS. SHE'S AN ABSOLUTE BEAR ABOUT OVERRUNS AND TARDINESS. LET'S KEEP HER!

DAVENPORT. As indispensable as sensible shoes.

PAID FOR BY HER CHUMS.

THAT'S IT? NOTHING ABOUT URINE SAMPLES?

I WARNED YOU SHE MIGHT TAKE THE HIGH ROAD.

CLI ☆☆

...AND I THINK IF WE CAN GET SOME CANVASSERS DOWN TO THE 5TH WARD...

SWEETEST! EXTRAORDINARY NEWS!

A BACHMAN'S WARBLER HAS BEEN SPOTTED OUT AT YOSEMITE! THROW ON A WRAP! I'VE GOT THE STUDEBAKER WARMED UP AND READY TO GO!

UM... I'M AFRAID I CAN'T GO OUT BIRD-WATCHING WITH YOU TODAY, DICK.

EGADS! WHY NOT?

I'M RUNNING FOR CONGRESS, DEAR.

I GUESS YOU DIDN'T HEAR ME. I SAID, A BACHMAN'S WARBLER!

THANKS FOR BEING HERE, RICK. IT'LL MEAN A LOT TO LACEY.

HOW'S SHE HOLDING UP?

NOT SO WELL. SHE'S FEELING TERRIBLY GUILTY THAT SHE WASN'T WITH DICK AT THE TIME.

AND NOW SHE'S GOT TO GET THROUGH THIS MEMORIAL SERVICE WITH ALL OF DICK'S BIRDING BUDDIES.

MRS. D? I BROUGHT YOU A PEPPERMINT. OOPS, ALL I'VE GOT IS STRING!

JEREMY! COME QUICKLY! I FOUND A REALLY GOOD PEW!

©B Trudeau

WE SHALL NOW HEAR A FEW WORDS FROM SOME OF DICK'S FRIENDS.

THAD UP FIRST! JEREMY ON DECK!

ME? GOOD GRAVY!

SHOULDN'T JEREMY GO FIRST, REG? HE HAS SENIORITY.

QUITE RIGHT! CAN WE CHANGE THE BATTING ORDER, PADRE?

I CAN'T FOLLOW JEREMY. HE'S TOO ELECTRIFYING!

GOOD POINT. OKAY, THAD, YOU'RE ON AS SCHEDULED!

HE CAN'T. HE'S STILL PRAYING.

NO, I'M LOOKING FOR MY GLASSES. YOU BETTER GO FIRST, JEREMY!

WILL SOMEBODY GET UP THERE?

HEAR, HEAR!

ISN'T THAT THE WIDOW?

FOUND 'EM!

©B Trudeau

WHEN ONE THINKS OF RICHARD WINDAMERE DAVENPORT, ONE THINKS OF A MAN WHOSE NAME WAS ALMOST SYNONYMOUS WITH THE BUFF-BREASTED FLYCATCHER.

WHY? WHY NOT BENDIRE'S THRASHER OR THE BRISTLE-THIGHED CURLEW? GOOD QUESTION. I RANG UP DICK'S SCHOOLMATE CECIL TO SEE IF HE KNEW, BUT HE WAS OUT WEEDING.

VINTAGE CECIL! IF IT'S NOT ONE THING WITH HIM, CHANCES ARE VERY GOOD INDEED IT'S ANOTHER. THE STORIES I COULD TELL YOU ABOUT THAT CHARACTER!

BUT I DIGRESS...

NOT AT ALL! CARRY ON, OLD BOY!

YES, TELL, TELL!

©B Trudeau

...AND EVEN THOUGH DICK WAS TWICE ELECTED PRESIDENT OF THE MARYLAND AUDUBON SOCIETY, HE NEVER ABUSED THAT POSITION OR PUT ON AIRS.

HOW BEST TO HONOR OUR FALLEN COLLEAGUE? AFTER PUTTING ON OUR THINKING CAPS, WE IN THE SOCIETY CAME UP WITH A TRIBUTE WE THINK IS FITTING.

FOR THE NEXT MINUTE, IN AN ORNITHOLOGISTS' SALUTE, WE WILL ALL PERFORM OUR FAVORITE BIRD CALLS. EVERYONE READY? ...ALTOGETHER!

HONK! HONK! CAW! QUACK! CHEE WICKY! CHEE! PLAAT! PLAAT! CHIRP!

I DON'T KNOW HOW MUCH MORE OF THIS I CAN TAKE.

©B Trudeau

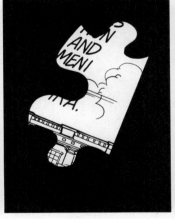

GUYS! UNSCRAMBLE THE IRAN CRISIS PUZZLE...

WELL, DAVID, I 'VLVE

IMPRESS CHICKS! WOW BUSINESS ASSOCIATES!

SOME MORE PIECES OF THE IRANSCAM PUZZLE EMERGE...

MK-ING SPECIAL H...

TOMORROW: THE CRISIS REVEALED!

THE PUZZLE COMES TOGETHER.

PRESIDENT. AS YOUR DR. I COU KNO

Title: "MISTAKES WERE Scene: 087

NOT A VERY PRETTY PICTURE, IS IT? I'M ROLAND HEDLEY. COURAGE.

GOTTA GO. SEE YOU TONIGHT.

HOLD IT, RICK. YOU'RE SUPPOSED TO DRIVE JEFF TO DAY CARE TODAY.

OH, HEY, SORRY, I CAN'T, BABE. I'VE GOT A BIG MEETING TODAY AND...

SO DO I. IN FACT, I USUALLY DO. FOR ONCE, I'D LIKE TO ARRIVE ON TIME!

YOU DON'T UNDER-STAND, JOANIE. MY EDITOR'S OUT SICK, SO I...

RICK, YOU PROMISED TO TAKE HIM! YOU ALWAYS DO THIS TO ME!

YO! DADDY! I'LL WALK.

COULD YOU, SON?

RICK!

AT THE RISK OF SOUNDING POST-FEMINIST, RICK, IT'S JUST NOT WORKING. WITH BOTH OF US PURSUING CAREERS, JEFF IS BEING CHEATED!

MAYBE IT'S DIFFERENT WITH OTHER PEOPLE, BUT IT'S FINALLY BEGINNING TO GET TO ME. SOMETHING HAS GOT TO GIVE HERE!

I WANT TO PROPOSE SOMETHING. YOU PROBABLY WON'T GO FOR IT, BUT I THINK...

HEY, DON'T WORRY ABOUT ME, BABE. YOU DO WHAT YOU HAVE TO DO.

I THINK YOU SHOULD QUIT YOUR JOB.

YOU CAN ALWAYS GO BACK TO WORK AFTER...SAY WHAT?

QUIT MY *JOB?* C'MON, JOANIE, GET SERIOUS.

OKAY, HOW ABOUT WORKING AT HOME, THEN? THIS IS IMPORTANT, RICK.

THEN WHY DON'T *YOU* DO IT?

IT'S NOT AS PRACTICAL. C'MON, RICK, YOU'RE THE ONE WHO WROTE ABOUT THE NEW BREED OF COMMITTED FATHERS!

RIGHT, AS A DETACHED REPORTER.

HUH?

I WASN'T ACTUALLY INVOLVED, JOANIE. IT WOULDN'T HAVE BEEN PROFESSIONAL.

I DON'T KNOW, JOANIE. I'M NOT SURE I CAN GET ANY REAL WORK DONE AT HOME.

IT'S WORTH A TRY, RICK. I'D DO IT IF I COULD.

WELL...OKAY. I'LL SPEAK TO CHARLIE ABOUT IT.

GOOD!

MOMMY!

ALTHOUGH I'M NOT CONVINCED THIS IS REALLY NECESS...

WHAT IS IT, JEFF?

MOMMY, HAVE YOU SEEN DADDY?

THAT'S ENOUGH, HONEY. WE'RE ON IT.

HEY, CHARLIE, I WONDER IF IT'D BE OKAY IF I HOOKED UP A COMPUTER MODEM AND WORKED AT HOME FOR AWHILE?

HUH?

JOANIE THINKS JEFF ISN'T SEEING ENOUGH OF HIS PARENTS. WE DECIDED I SHOULD START TAKING CARE OF HIM DURING THE DAY.

HEE, HEE!

CHARLIE, THIS IS THE '80s. SPARE ME THE...

HOUSE-WIMP! HOUSE-WIMP!

Panel 1: MOM, YOU DON'T REALLY BELIEVE ORAL ROBERTS WILL DIE IF HE DOESN'T GET THE MONEY, DO YOU?
I DON'T KNOW, MIKEY...

Panel 2: I DO KNOW THAT IF GOD CALLS ORAL HOME, THERE WILL BE MILLIONS OF PEOPLE KICKING THEMSELVES FOR NOT HEEDING HIS WARNING.

Panel 3: WE CAN'T STAND IDLY BY, MIKEY. THE EYES OF THE WORLD ARE NOW ON OKLAHOMA!

Panel 4: HI! IT'S DAY 32 ON THE ORAL ROBERTS DEATH WATCH! FOR AN UPDATE ON GOD'S DEMANDS, LET'S GO TO TULSA!

Panel 5: WELCOME BACK TO DAY 32 OF THE ORAL ROBERTS DEATH WATCH! MY PRODUCER JAKE AND I ARE STILL TALKING ABOUT GOD'S EXTRAORDINARY $4.5 MILLION SHAKEDOWN.

Panel 6: JAKE, I THINK WHAT CONCERNS ME MOST IS THE CLAIM THAT GOD IS HOLDING A LIFE HOSTAGE FOR FUND-RAISING PURPOSES, THAT HE IS, IN EFFECT, A COMMON TERRORIST.

Panel 7: AS ONE OBSERVER HAS PUT IT, "NO CAUSE CAN JUSTIFY TERRORISM. IT IS THE CRIME OF COWARDS. TERRORISM IS HEINOUS AND INTOLERABLE!"
WHO SAID THAT?

Panel 8: RONALD REAGAN.
STRONG STUFF. BUT WOULDN'T GOD KNOW HE DOESN'T MEAN IT?

Panel 9: ORAL ROBERTS DEATH WATCH, YOU'RE ON THE AIR!
YEAH, I AGREE WE SHOULDN'T CAVE IN TO GOD'S ULTIMATUMS.

Panel 10: OTHERWISE, WHERE'S IT GONNA STOP? IF WE PAY $4.5 MILLION TO SAVE ROBERTS, NEXT THING YOU KNOW, WE'LL BE COUGHING UP $5 MILLION FOR WOODY ALLEN, OR $10 MILLION FOR JERRY GARCIA.

Panel 11: IT COULD JUST GET OUT OF HAND, YOU KNOW? I MEAN, HOW MUCH DO YOU SUPPOSE GOD COULD GET FOR SOMEONE LIKE VANNA WHITE?

Panel 12: GOD ONLY KNOWS.
EXACTLY! HE'D HAVE US OVER A BARREL!

Panel 13: WE'RE BACK, AND FIELDING CALLS...
...WITH JUST TWO MINUTES LEFT IN DAY 32 OF THE ORAL ROBERTS DEATH WATCH!

Panel 14: GO AHEAD, YOU'RE ON THE AIR!
YEAH, I THINK Y'ALL SHOULD BE COOL. NO WAY GOD'S GONNA PUT OUT BROTHER ORAL'S LIGHTS, DIG?

Panel 15: GOD'S JUST WORKIN' A MEGA-EVENT, TO GET HIS PEOPLE INVOLVED IN A GOOD CAUSE! IT'S LIKE A COMBINATION OF THE "WE ARE THE WORLD" AND THE "HANDS" PROJECTS.

Panel 16: AS IN, "HE'S GOT THE WHOLE WORLD IN HIS HANDS"?
RIFF ON, MY MAN!
IT'S NOW DAY 33...

I CAN'T GET OVER HOW OPEN THIS STATE IS TO NEW IDEAS, B.D. – THIS TASK FORCE IS JUST THE BEGINNING!

I'M SURE IT WON'T BE LONG BEFORE WE'RE EVEN STUDYING THINGS LIKE REINCARNATION.

SOMETHING ELSE YOU BELIEVE IN, NO DOUBT.

ABSOLUTELY. THAT'S WHY I DON'T CARE IF I'M A REAL SUCCESSFUL FILM ACTRESS. IN MY NEXT LIFE, I'LL BE SOMEONE ENTIRELY DIFFERENT!

LIKE WHO?

I DUNNO. MAYBE SOMEONE IN THE RECORDING INDUSTRY.

OKAY, THAT'S ENOUGH SUN FOR TODAY.

BUT THE BEST THING ABOUT THE STUDY GROUP, B.D., IS THAT IT'S A LEGITIMIZATION OF THE NEW AGE CULTURE — ITS LIFE-STYLE, ITS PHILOSOPHY, ITS LITERATURE, EVEN ITS MUSIC!

NEW AGE HAS ITS OWN MUSIC?

OH, YES, AND IT'S WONDERFUL. HEARING IT IS LIKE FLOATING IN A WARM SOUND BATH. IT TOTALLY FREES THE MIND!

OBVIOUSLY. LOOK, BOOPSIE, DO ME A FAVOR AND DON'T BRING ANY OF THIS STUFF HOME, OKAY?

YOU SILLY! YOU'VE BEEN LISTENING TO IT FOR THE LAST THREE HOURS!

HUH?

NON-INTRUSIVE, ISN'T IT? THIS PIECE IS CALLED "AIR PUDDING."

I'D LIKE TO CALL TO ORDER THIS FIRST MEETING OF THE CALIFORNIA TASK FORCE TO PROMOTE SELF-ESTEEM AND PERSONAL AND SOCIAL RESPONSIBILITY!

AS YOU KNOW, OUR MANDATE IS NOTHING LESS THAN TO STUDY THE RELATIONSHIP BETWEEN SELF-ESTEEM AND SOCIAL PROBLEMS, AND TO IDENTIFY PROGRAMS THAT ADDRESS THAT RELATIONSHIP!

OKAY, BEFORE WE ROLL UP OUR SLEEVES, LET ME FIRST JUST ASK HOW EVERYONE HERE FEELS ABOUT HIMSELF TODAY.

GOOD. GOOD. GOOD. GOOD. GOOD! GOOD. GOOD, GOOD.

...AND I'VE ALSO DONE EXTENSIVE RESEARCH ON CAUSES OF TEEN DELINQUENCY.

THANK YOU, DOCTOR. WELL, BARBARA ANN, THAT JUST LEAVES YOU!

HI, EVERYONE. I'M BARBARA ANN BOOPSTEIN. I'M AN ACTRESS, A SPIRITUAL VOYAGER, AND A CHANNELER WHO SPEAKS FOR A REALLY GOOD-LOOKING 21,355-YEAR-OLD WARRIOR NAMED HUNK-RA!

DOES THAT MEAN HE'S ON THE TASK FORCE, TOO?

UM... LET ME CHECK THE BYLAWS. I KNOW HE CAN'T VOTE.

WITH THE CURRENT EMPHASIS ON SAFE WHOOPEE, MY PERSONAL VIEW IS THAT THE NETWORKS WILL SOON RELENT AND PERMIT ADVERTISING OF THIS KIND.

2-24

HOWEVER, OUR CLIENT UNDERSTANDS THAT SOME VIEWERS MAY FIND THE MERE MENTION OF ITS PRODUCT ON TELEVISION OFFENSIVE.

FOR THAT REASON, OUR CAMPAIGN WILL REFER TO THE PRODUCT BY A CODE WORD THAT IS ENTIRELY UNRELATED IN MEANING, BUT WHICH WILL SUBLIMINALLY ALERT THE MATURE VIEWER.

THAT WORD IS "CONDO."

WHOA! SAFE BY A WHISKER!

GOT MY ATTENTION!

WHY PICK THE UNRELATED WORD "CONDO" TO REFER TO THE UNMENTIONABLE PRODUCT WE ARE SELLING? BEAR WITH ME FOR A TALE ABOUT MY TEEN-AGE KID...

"A DRUGSTORE, LATE LAST YEAR..."

UH... EXCUSE ME?

WHAT CAN I DO FOR YOU, SON?

UM... WELL, I'D LIKE... UH... THAT IS... UH... I'D... I'D...

YES?

I'D LIKE A LARGE CONDO.

THEN YOU BETTER START SAVING NOW.

OKAY, WE OPEN ON A COUPLE OF Y-PEOPLE READING THE SUNDAY PAPER IN THEIR DUPLEX...

TITLE: "SAFE WHOOPEE"

Young couple in their apartment.

THEY LOOK UP AT THE SAME TIME AND EXCHANGE KNOWING, ROMANTIC GLANCES...

Exchange glance

AS HE GETS UP TO DIM THE LIGHTS, SHE SAYS, "DARLING, LET'S BE SURE TO USE A CONDOMINIUM!" CUT TO PRODUCT NAME AND OUT!

he: "Ha"

WHAT DO YOU THINK?

NOT BELIEVABLE.

YEAH, YUPS SCHEDULE EVERYTHING.

OH, BRAD, MAYBE YOU'RE RIGHT! MAYBE WE ARE FINALLY READY!

WELL, WE HAVE BEEN TOGETHER FOR NINE YEARS, DARLING.

OKAY, BUT REMEMBER, WE HAVE TO PRACTICE SAFE WHOOPEE!

OF COURSE, BRENDA, OF COURSE!

HAVE YOU GOT A CONDOMINIUM, DARLING?

I'LL... I'LL CHECK MY WALLET!

CUT!

SLOW IT DOWN, KIDS! WE'RE NOT DOING FEDERAL EXPRESS HERE!

BRAD, CHANGE "WALLET" TO "MEDICINE CABINET."

GOOD EVENING. FOR FOUR MONTHS NOW, WASHINGTON HAS BEEN MESMERIZED BY THE PRESIDENT'S EFFORTS TO REMEMBER HIS ROLE IN THE IRANIAN AFFAIR.

CAN THESE MEMORIES EVER BE RETRIEVED? DO THEY IN FACT EXIST? FOLLOW ALONG AS WE TRY TO BRING 'EM BACK ALIVE IN...

L. DUCK

THE RETURN TO REAGAN'S BRAIN!

WHO? WHAT? WHEN?

THWITT!

MARCH 24, 1987– IT'S BEEN SEVEN YEARS SINCE MY LAST TREK THROUGH REAGAN'S BRAIN...

WHAT A BLEAK, RAVAGED LANDSCAPE GREETS US. CRANIAL COILS LAY HEAPED IN LIFELESS DISARRAY.

NEURONS ARE STRETCHED AND FRAYED, THEIR DENDRITIC SPINES WORN AWAY.

IN SHORT, NOTHING HAS CHANGED.

SEE? MY INITIALS!

R&H '80

MARCH 25 – PROGRESS UP THE BRAIN STEM IS MADDENINGLY SLOW. SLUDGE SLIDES BLOCK OUR WAY AT EVERY TURN.

FINALLY, WE GAIN A MESA OVERLOOKING A SWELTERING MASS OF NEURONS.

SHERPA!

SIRE?

WHAT PLACE IS THIS?

IT IS KNOWN AS THE CEREBRUM, SAHIB. IT IS WHERE THE PRESIDENT DOES ALL HIS CRITICAL THINKING.

SOUNDS PEACEFUL ENOUGH.

SHOULD WE SET UP THE BASE CAMP, SAHIB?

MARCH 26 – TODAY WE MAKE OUR FINAL ASSAULT ON THE FORNIX, REAGAN'S MEMORY VAULT.

THE APPROACH IS ARDUOUS. NEURAL PASSAGES ARE SHRUNKEN AND CALCIFIED FROM CHRONIC DISUSE.

SUDDENLY...

LIVE SYNAPSE!

CRAK!

WE LOSE A PORTER.

POOR DEVIL...

HE KNEW THE RISKS. PUSH ON, LADS!

APRIL 1— I PUSH ON. REAGAN'S MEMORY OF IRANGATE HAS BECOME MY HOLY GRAIL. BUT PROVISIONS SPENT, I GROW FAINT FROM HUNGER.

I RECALL SOMETHING MY SHERPA SAID ABOUT THE MICRO-ORGANISMS FOUND IN THE CRANIUM BEING HIGH IN PROTEIN.

I EAT MY BELT.

APRIL 2, 1987— BREAKTHROUGH! A ROUTINE CORE SAMPLE TAPS INTO A VEIN OF HIDDEN MEMORY!

GOOD GOD... IT EXISTS!

YES, BURIED BENEATH THE STRATA OF CONSCIOUS THOUGHT IS A MOTHERLODE OF SUPPRESSED MEMORIES. I AM SUDDENLY FACED WITH A MONSTROUS DILEMMA!

DO I BRING THIS IMPACTED INFORMATION TO THE SURFACE WHERE THE PRESIDENT CAN ACCESS IT? IS IT PROPER FOR A JOURNALIST TO PLAY SUCH A ROLE?

I AGONIZE OVER IT FOR DAYS.

WHAT WOULD BARBARA WALTERS DO?

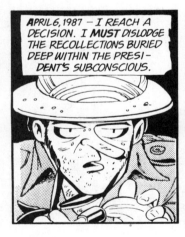

APRIL 6, 1987— I REACH A DECISION. I MUST DISLODGE THE RECOLLECTIONS BURIED DEEP WITHIN THE PRESIDENT'S SUBCONSCIOUS.

FASHIONING A CRUDE INCENDIARY DEVICE FROM A BRANDY BOTTLE, I LET FLY.

KA-WHAM!

A RUSH OF MEMORY, SIR? ABOUT WHAT?   I FORGET.

MR. & MRS. SHE-MOMMY

WHA... WHO... >GASP!< WHO ARE YOU?   MEDEVAC, MR. HEDLEY. JUST TAKE IT EASY. WE'RE GETTING YOU OUT OF HERE.

YOU'RE A LUCKY MAN. WE SPOTTED THE SMOKE IN THE CORTEX. OKAY! PULL HIM UP!

THAT WAS QUITE SOME STUNT YOU PULLED, PAL. IT RELEASED A FLOOD OF MEMORIES FOR THE PRESIDENT.

THE...THE MISSING PIECES?

AFRAID NOT. MOSTLY BASEBALL SCORES FROM THE '30s.

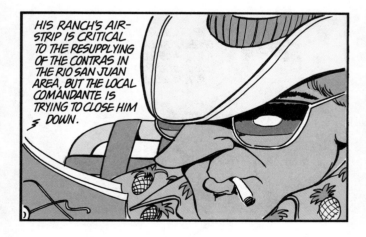

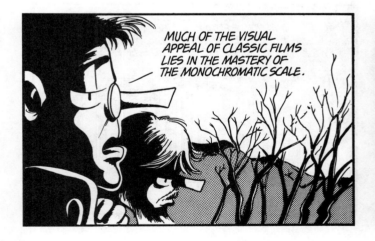

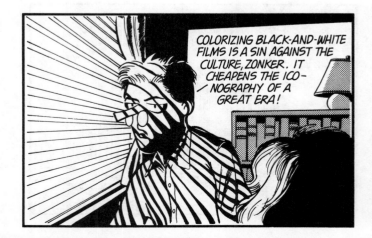

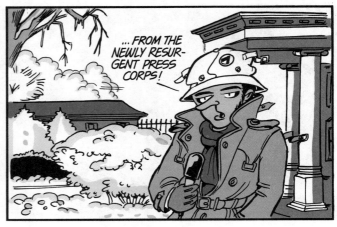

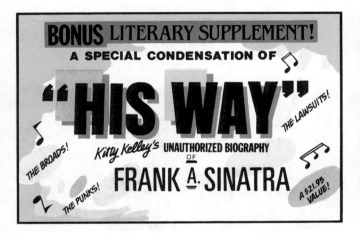

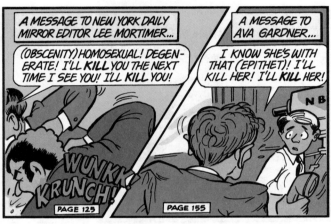

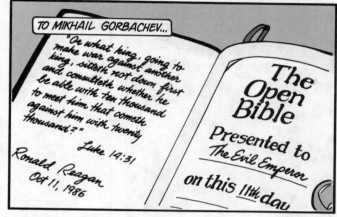

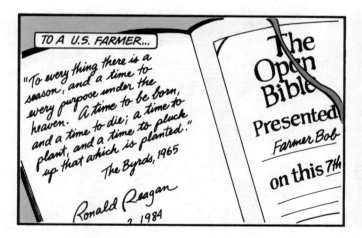

Constitution of the United States
The Original 7 Articles

PREAMBLE

We, the people of the United States, in order to form a more perfect Union, establish justice, insure domestic tranquility, provide for the common defense, promote the general welfare, and secure the blessings of liberty to ourselves and our posterity do ordain and establish this Constitution for the United States of America.

ARTICLE I.

Section 1—Legislative powers; in whom vested:

All legislative powers herein granted shall be vested in a Congress of the United States, which shall consist of a Senate and House of Representatives.

Section 2—House of Representatives, how and by whom chosen. Qualifications of a Representative. Representatives and direct taxes, how apportioned. Enumeration. Vacancies to be filled. Power of choosing officers, and of impeachment.

[Constitution text continues in multiple columns through Articles I–VII, including the signatures of George Washington and other delegates.]

ARTICLE II.

Section 1—President: his term in office. Electors of President; number and how appointed.

ARTICLE III.

Section 1—Judicial powers, Tenure, Compensation.

ARTICLE IV.

Section 1

ARTICLE V.

Constitution; how amended; proviso.

ARTICLE VI.

ARTICLE VII.

What ratification shall establish Constitution.

Done in convention by the unanimous consent of the States present the Seventeenth day of September in the year of our Lord one thousand seven hundred and eighty seven, and of the independence of the United States of America the Twelfth. In witness whereof we have hereunto subscribed our names.

George Washington. John Langdon. Nicholas Gilman. George Read. Rufus King. Wm. Saml. Johnson. Roger Sherman. Alexander Hamilton. Wil: Livingston. David Brearley. Wm. Paterson. Jona: Dayton. B. Franklin. Thomas Mifflin. Robt. Morris. Geo. Clymer. Thos. FitzSimons. Jared Ingersoll. James Wilson. Gouv. Morris. Geo: Read. Gunning Bedford Jun. John Dickinson. Richard Bassett. Jaco: Broom. James McHenry. Daniel of Saint Thomas' Jenifer. Danl. Carroll. John Blair. James Madison Jr. Wm. Blount. Rich'd. Dobbs Spaight. Hugh Williamson. J. Rutledge. Charles Cotesworth Pinckney. Charles Pinckney. Pierce Butler. William Few. Abr. Baldwin. Attest: William Jackson, Secretary.

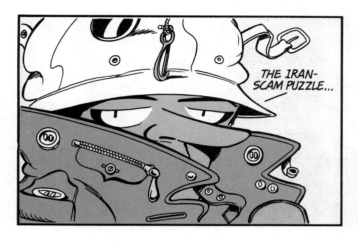

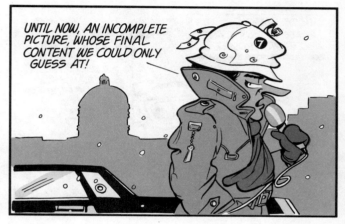

THE "DR. WHOOPEE" TEAM... WORKING FOR YOU!

COUNT ON IT!

EMPLOYEE-OF-THE-MONTH SAL DOONESBURY TALKS ABOUT "DR. WHOOPEE"...

THE JOB ISN'T REALLY ABOUT MARKET SHARE — IT'S ABOUT PEOPLE, AND SOLVING THEIR PROBLEMS...

LAST MONTH I GOT AN URGENT CALL FROM A LARGE SORORITY AT A WELL-KNOWN EASTERN COLLEGE. SPRING BREAK WAS 12 HOURS AWAY, AND THEY NEEDED PROTECTION.

"I QUICKLY ROUTED THE ORDER ONTO OUR PRIORITY SATELLITE LINE, INSTANTLY ALERTING THE HOME OFFICE IN FLAGSTAFF..."

"WITHIN MINUTES, THE ORDER WAS PROCESSED AND LOADED AND WINGING ITS WAY TO THE ANXIOUS SORORITY SISTERS..."

'EVENING, MISS!

DOCTOR WHOOPEE! YOU MADE IT!

"DR. WHOOPEE," WHERE PEOPLE ARE JOB ONE.

SERVICE WITH A SMILE, NOT A SMIRK!